Being God's People

A Southern Baptist Church on Bold Mission

Robert A. Orr

Convention Press
Nashville, Tennessee

5160-05

This book is the text
for Course number 01020 in the subject area
"The Church" of the Church Study Course.

Dewey Decimal Classification Number: 262.7
Subject Heading: CHURCH

Printed in the United States of America.
Available from Baptist Book Stores.

Church Administration Department
The Sunday School Board of the Southern Baptist Convention
127 Ninth Avenue, North
Nashville, Tennessee 37234

Contents

Preface

Those of you who have read *A Church on Mission: an Intentional Response to the Needs of the Eighties* compiled by Reginald McDonough will notice that many sections of this book are similar to material in that one. The reason is that both books were written to communicate the heart of an internal reference document developed by Southern Baptist Convention agencies to describe their common understandings about the nature and work of a church and its programs.

This book is based on a 1986 update of the 1979 document that was the basis for *A Church on Mission*. Large portions of the 1979 material were unchanged in the update. Earlier books based on similar understandings among Southern Baptist agencies were *A Dynamic Church* in 1969 and *A Church Organized and Functioning* in 1963, both by W. L. Howse and W. O. Thomason.

This fourth book in the series, though presenting much of the same material, is intended to focus even greater emphasis on evangelism and missions as being at the heart of the mission of God's people and therefore of God's people called Southern Baptists. This was the main thrust of many of the revisions made in updating the agency reference document.

This book is intended to remind us that God expects His people to be effective in reaching out with the gospel. We must be if we are to turn the words *Bold Mission Thrust* into life-changing experiences, both in the lives of God's people and in the lives of the lost who need to hear the gospel through our efforts.

The first two chapters are foundational in thinking about the life and work of a Southern Baptist church on bold mission. As people committed to the Word of God, we turn to the Scriptures to review what God inspired His servants to record about the nature and mission of the church and about the nature and needs of persons who are to be reached with the gospel and helped to grow in the likeness of Christ. In considering the needs of persons, we also consider information from other sources.

Building on chapters 1 and 2, chapter 3 focuses on the mission, functions, and tasks (work to be done) by a church as God's people.

Being God's people means that we will be committed to knowing and doing His will for us in keeping with the opportunities and resources He makes available to us for our part in His redemptive mission.

Chapters 4 through 8 describe the basic programs of work as Southern Baptists have identified and learned to structure them through applying biblical teachings in practical experience, along with principles from other disciplines as God's Spirit has given guidance. In addition to discussing the two basic missions programs, Woman's Missionary Union and Brotherhood, chapter 8 also describes the Missions Development program, an emphasis program that has a new name and new tasks not found in *A Church on Mission.*

Chapter 9 emphasizes the major importance of evangelism in all church programs, especially the Sunday School and other basic programs which have tasks involving witness and ministry to the lost. In addition, it gives full treatment of the revised and expanded tasks and organization of the emphasis program of evangelism.

Chapter 10 presents the concerns of the other emphasis programs: family ministry, stewardship, vocational guidance, and the newly stated emphasis program of student ministry which was not in *A Church on Mission.*

Chapter 11 describes the contribution that service programs—media library, recreation services, and administrative services—can make toward helping God's people be effective in doing a church's work.

Chapter 12 discusses how the Church Council and related councils can help a church coordinate its programs to achieve maximum results from the efforts of God's people.

Southern Baptist Convention agencies use these understandings about a church and its programs as a basis for planning the assistance they offer to churches in the form of program suggestions curriculum and administrative materials, training events, and other services.

A concluding section encourages you as church leaders and members to evaluate your church program and its priorities in light of the biblical teachings about the nature and mission of God's people and Southern Baptists' stated commitment to reach every person on earth with the gospel by the year 2000—Bold Mission Thrust.

The writing is intentionally informal and conversational, as if we could just talk and think together about this important subject. I pray that God's Spirit will use this material to help you and your church as you shape your participation in God's mission. May your participation and mine be bold, effective, and all that God expects from us as His people. He is calling us to do much more than business as usual in our church life!

Introduction: God's People, the Church

This book is about God's people—those whom He has called according to His purpose to be brought into a saving relationship with Him through their faith in His only Son, Jesus Christ, and in that relationship to join Him in His mission of providing redemption for all humanity who will respond to Him in repentance and faith.

The Old Testament tells us of God's dealings with the people He called to be in covenant relationship with Him in order to bless all nations with the knowledge of God. When those He had called failed to honor the covenant and thus did not fulfill their role in His redemptive purpose, God provided a new covenant in Christ.

The New Testament tells us how God in love and grace provided this new covenant through His Son. All who will may participate in this new covenant by accepting Jesus Christ as Lord and Savior. The new covenant, like the old, carries with it both privilege and resonsibility. The responsibility is for God's people to share the message of redemption through Christ with people of all nations, creeds, and colors to the uttermost part of the earth, as our Lord commanded (see Matt. 28:19-20; Acts 1:8).

The New Testament records how God's people of the new covenant formed themselves into groups of believers—churches, God's "called-out ones"—in order to honor the covenant and share the message of God's love and redemption. Southern Baptists think of the church primarily as "a local body of baptized believers who are associated by covenant in the faith and fellowship of the gospel, observing the two ordinances of Christ, committed to His teachings, exercising the gifts, rights, and privileges invested in them by His Word, and seeking to extend the gospel to the ends of the earth."[1] They recognize that the New Testament also speaks of the church as the body of Christ which includes all the redeemed of all ages.

The title of this book, *Being God's People,* is intended to emphasize the truth that churches are made up of God's people of the new covenant and that the covenant involves both responsibilities and privileges. It was chosen to help us think of the church as God's people called to do God's work in the world under the lordship of Christ and in the power of the Holy Spirit. As churches, God's people worship, fellowship, and serve together in their efforts to express in daily living their commitment to the person and redemptive message of Jesus Christ, their Savior and Lord. Being God's people includes fulfilling the responsibilities of the covenant as well as enjoying its privileges.

As you read this book, let me ask you to join me in making a special effort to think of the church as God's people—believers like you and me—rather than as an "it"—an organization, a building, or a meeting. Also, let's make a special effort to think of the church as God's people when we are away from the church building, scattered in homes, workplaces, schools, and other activities. Much of our "church work" needs to be done away from our meetinghouse. As we go about our daily living, we are to witness and minister in the name of Christ.

The subtitle, *A Southern Baptist Church on Bold Mission* is intended to emphasize (1) that God's people who comprise each Southern Baptist church are called by Him to be on mission with Him in bringing redemption through Christ to all persons, and (2) that Southern Baptists who cooperate through the Southern Baptist Convention and its agencies have been challenged to participate in Bold Mission Thrust, an all-out effort by Soutern Baptist churches through both direct and cooperative efforts to reach every person on earth with the gospel by the year 2000.

When these words are published early in 1987, we Southern Baptists will have less than thirteen years remaining to work toward achieving this grand objective. As God's people called Southern Baptists, we need to devote ourselves as never before to reaching people, witnessing to them, ministering to them, and giving sacrificially of our resources to reach through cooperative efforts those we cannot reach directly. We need to become *bold* in sharing the gospel! Paul and Barnabus spoke boldly in the Lord (see Acts 14:3; 19:8). Apollos spoke boldly (see Acts 18:26). Paul asked the Ephesians to pray that he might open his mouth boldly to make known the mystery of the gospel (see Eph. 6:19). We must demonstrate in our lives the conviction Paul expressed in Romans 1:16: "For I am not ashamed of the gospel of Christ: for it is the power of God unto salvation to every one that believeth." Our Lord said that the power we need to be bold would come from the Holy Spirit, and He promised to be with us as we share in His mission.

Have you and your church caught the vision of what needs to be accomplished, of what can be accomplished in the power of the Holy Spirit if God's people will it to be so? In your fellowship of believers, is there a growing sense of urgency about reaching the lost and ministering in Christ's name? These are questions I have asked myself while writing this book. I ask you to consider them seriously and prayerfully as you read the pages that follow.

May God's Spirit help all of us Southern Baptists understand fully and respond unreservedly to the great opportunity He has given us. When have we had more resources to bring to our mission—more members, more churches, more money, more effective communications media, more trained and dedicated leaders, more cooperative work by denominational agencies to support the churches' efforts and to represent them in cooperative missions? Surely God will hold us accountable for our use of all He has entrusted to us! Are we ready to face His penetrating questions about our stewardship of life and all other resources? Please join me in thinking about that question as you continue reading.

---

[1]*The Baptist Faith and Message: a Statement Adopted by the Southern Baptist Convention* (Nashville: Sunday School Board of the Southern Baptist Convention, 1963), pp. 12-13.

CHAPTER 1

Learning from Churches in the New Testament

Southern Baptists have characteristically looked to the Bible as their guide for faith and practice. We look to God's inspired Word to learn what He expects His people to be and to do. By studying what biblical writers recorded about the nature and purpose of the churches in New Testament times, we find guidance for our churches.

If someone asked you to define *church*, what would you say? Compare your definition with the one in the introduction which is taken from *The Baptist Faith and Message* statement adopted by the Southern Baptist Convention in 1963. Though we recognize that statement as a biblically based summary of beliefs that many if not most Southern Baptists hold in common, our authority for faith and practice is the Bible itself, interpreted by each believer and each church through the guidance of the Holy Spirit.

The Bible contains truths and principles about the nature of a church which are called biblical foundations. God's people need a thorough understanding of these foundational truths as a guide to being on God's mission in the contemporary world. But if we look into the New Testament to find one brief, comprehensive definition of the church in any one reference, we will look in vain. That is why the definition in *The Baptist Faith and Message* is based on the many references listed after it.

In making our study of biblical teachings about the church, we must ask the Spirit's help in avoiding either of two crucial mistakes: (1) reading our own preconceived ideas and current practices into the Scriptures, and (2) ignoring or trying to explain away any of the truths God has preserved for us in the written Word.

The Nature and Mission of God's People, the Church

The nature and mission of God's people grow out of the nature and mission of God. He has chosen to reveal Himself through nature, through the Bible, and most fully through the person and work of Jesus Christ. Through this self-revelation He has made it clear that in His love and mercy He is working to redeem His creation from the devastating effects of human sin. With that in mind, *mission* may be defined as God's work of redeeming His creation in Jesus Christ, a task which He calls His people—every church—to share.[1] Mission is God's work. When He calls persons to be on mission, He sends them to join Him where He is already present and at work. The mission of God's people, therefore, in the great variety of the corporate life of the churches and in the power of the Holy Spirit, is to show the world what God has done, is doing, and promises to do in Jesus Christ. It is to participate in God's mission which centers in Christ.

How well does this statement of mission describe how you and your church think of your mission in the world?

New Testament Descriptions of the Church

The inspired New Testament writers used several descriptive terms to set in focus the essential nature of the church. The title of this book is based on one of them.

The Church—God's People
The people of God.—New Testament writers sometimes referred to the church as "the people of God," meaning a fellowship of persons made one under God's kingly rule.[2] In describing the people of God in Christ, they used terms that were originally applied to Israel, the people associated with God's redemptive purpose. The church is "the Israel of God" (Gal. 6:16), "Abraham's offspring" (Gal. 3:29, RSV),[3] "a chosen race, a royal priesthood, a holy nation, God's own people" (1 Pet. 2:9, RSV; see Ex. 19:6).

The called-out ones.—The New Testament Greek word usually translated into English as *church* is *ekklesia.* In the Septuagint, the Greek translation of the Old Testament, this word translates the Hebrew term *qahal* which referred to the nation of Israel assembled before God, and so designated the people of God under divine rule (see Deut. 31:30).

The concept of the called-out ones is found in both the Old and New Testaments as a reference to the ones chosen by God to be His emissaries (i.e., "a light to the nations," Isa. 49:6, RSV; "the light of the world," Matt. 5:14). God's people were called out for a mission that included more than enjoying fellowship with God and with one another.

In the New Testament *ekklesia* is used to refer to "called out ones." Among the Greeks the term meant an assembly of the people called out from their homes into some public place for the purpose of deliberating. Though the term is used in some passages in a general way to include all persons redeemed by Christ and made one in the family of God (see Matt. 16:18; Eph. 3:21; 5:23-25,29,32; Col. 1:18; Heb. 12:23), the New Testament writers most frequently refer to the church as a local body, a fellowship of baptized believers voluntarily associated with one another in the faith and fellowship of the gospel, committed to Christ's teachings, and seeking to extend the gospel to the ends of the earth.[4] Thus we find references to the church of Jerusalem, the church at Antioch, the church at Rome, and the churches of Galatia (a province, not a city).

Those sent.—Our understanding of the church is enriched and expanded by studying New Testament use of the Greek verb *apostellein* meaning "to send" and the related noun *apostolos* meaning "one sent." These words carry the strong religious meaning of ambassadorial authority. The authority for the mission of the believer *(apostolos)* comes from the sender, God. Every member of the church is an apostle in this sense; every believer is sent by God. Jesus said that the mission of His followers was similar to His own in that He sent them in much the same way He Himself was sent (see John 17:8). It is the nature of God's people in a church to be the sent ones—to proclaim, witness, and minister.

The nature of the Christian gospel is evangelistic and missionary. In principle, the church that is alive must evangelize (see Matt. 28:19-20; Acts 1:8). If God's people are to be true to their commission—God's mission, the whole world is their field (see Matt. 13:38).[5]

Other Biblical Descriptions of the Church

The church of God (see 1 Cor. 1:2; 10:32; 11:22; 15:9; 2 Cor. 1:1; Gal. 1:13; 1 Tim. 3:5) or *the churches of God* (1 Cor. 11:16; 1 Thess. 2:14; 2 Thess. 1:4).—These expressions reflect the idea that the church belongs to the Lord Himself (see Acts 20:28; Matt. 16:18).

A fellowship of believers empowered by the Holy Spirit.—The distinctive New Testament word for fellowship is *koinonia*. This Greek word means "sharing, participation, communion, fellowship." *Koinonia* is not a human creation but the gift of God, the product of a relationship with Him (see 1 John 1:3). The Book of Acts describes the close-knit fellowship of God's people in the Jerusalem church, the "togetherness" of the members in prayer (see Acts 1:14; 2:1), worship (see Acts 2:46), ministry (see Acts 5:12), benevolent acts (see Acts 2:44-45; 4:32-37), and sharing the gospel (see Acts 5:42). *Koinonia* should be a strong distinguishing characteristic of the people of God in every church (see 1 John 1:7).

A new humanity.—This is another expression Paul used to picture God's people as God's creation through Christ. The church consists of diverse groups that formerly were set against one another (see Eph. 2:14-20; Gal. 6:15).

The body of Christ.—Paul used this phrase most frequently to describe the church (see Rom. 12:4-5; 1 Cor. 12:12-27; Eph. 1:22-23; 2:14-16; 3:3-13; 4:1-16; 5:30; Col. 1:18,24; 2:16-19; 3:15). From his statements we may draw several conclusions about the church:

• Jesus Christ is the head, and the only head, of the church.

• Members of a church are members because of their intimate relationship with Him.

• The purpose of the church is to carry out the will of Christ which He purposed in His heart before He came to earth.

• Like members of the physical body, members of Christ's body, the church, have a wide variety of responsibilities to carry out, both individually and collectively.

• Each member has his or her own particular and individual gifts, yet all members are interrelated and need one another.

• Although the members have various gifts, real and vital unity is found in the body of Christ.

God's flock.—This expression is used in both the Old and New Testaments to describe God's people (see Isa. 40:11; Ps. 23). Jesus referred to His followers in that way (see Matt. 26:31; Luke 12:32; John 10:16; 21:15-17).

Branches of the Vine.—This expression was used by our Lord to communicate how His people are related to Him. Drawing from Old Testament symbols, he said, "I am the vine, you are the branches" (John 15:5, RSV). Other passages indicate that He expects the branches to be in fruitful relationship with Him.

God's family.—Though the Scriptures do not specifically refer to the church as a family, the language of filial relationships is used in the Scriptures to describe our relationship with Christ. Those who receive Christ become children of God (see John 1:12). Christ's family are the ones who do the will of God (see Mark 3:33-35). Those who are led by the Spirit of God are His sons (see Rom. 8:14). The Holy Spirit assures us of our family relationship (see Rom. 8:16).

The bride of Christ.—Still another family-oriented phrase used in the New Testament describes the church (see 2 Cor. 11:2-3; Eph. 5:25-32; Rev. 19:7-9; 21:9). The Gospels complete the analogy by depicting Christ as a bridegroom (see Matt. 22:2; 25:1-13; Mark 2:18-20; Luke 14:7-11; John 3:25-29). As with a wholesome marital relationship, the relationship between Christ and His people is one of love and fidelity.

God's field.—Paul also used this expression to describe the church (see 1 Cor. 3:9) as a garden plot under God's cultivation for the purpose of bearing fruit.

God's building.—Paul used this expression (see 1 Cor. 3:9) to refer to the church as a building being constructed according to His plan. He also described the church as a temple or sanctuary (see 1 Cor. 3:16) whose chief cornerstone is Jesus Christ "in whom all the building fitly framed together groweth unto an holy temple in the Lord" (Eph. 2:21). God builds His church out of living persons redeemed by His grace. The result is "a spiritual house" (1 Pet. 2:5) wherein God is pleased to dwell. His presence makes possible and necessary a holy people (see 1 Cor. 3:17).

Pillar and bulwark of the truth.—This is what the "church of the living God" is to be (1 Tim. 3:15). These words designate the church as key witness to the truth of God's revelation. Also, they suggest the church's role in supporting and defending the truth (see 1 Pet. 3:15-16; Jude 3; 1 Tim. 4:13).

The Divine Origin and Relationships of the Church

According to the New Testament the church originated in the mind of God and was created to serve His purposes, as shown in the verses that have been referenced. Jesus said, "I will build my church" (Matt. 16:18). In this passage the word *ekklesia* is used in its universal sense.

The church is a divine institution because of its relationships. First, there is the relationship to God as seen in Paul's expressions like "the church of God" (1 Cor. 10:32; 11:22; 15:9), "all God's beloved in Rome" (Rom. 1:7, RSV), "fellow citizens with the saints and members of the household of God" (Eph. 2:19, RSV). Peter dealt extensively with the church's distinctive relationship to God (see 1 Pet. 1:3 to 2:10). First Peter 2:4-10 grounds the doctrine of the priesthood of all believers in this divine ownership.

Second, the church is divine because of its relationship to Jesus Christ, the Founder (see Matt. 16:18) and Head of the church (see Col. 1:18; Eph. 1:22-23; 4:15; 5:23). The church is like a body to the Head and must function accordingly (see 1 Cor. 6:15-20; 10:14-22; 11:28-34; 12:12,14; Rom. 7:4; 12:5; Col. 1:24; 3:15). The proof of this relationship is in the fruit produced as a result of the connection with the Life Source—the Head, Jesus Christ—just as fruit on branches shows they are productively related to the vine.

Third, the church is divine because of its relationship to the Holy Spirit. The Spirit directed the witnessing of the disciples at Pentecost and brought to Christ the three thousand persons who were added to the church (see Acts 2:4,38,41). By the Holy Spirit's power the church maintains its life and growth. The Spirit was at work in the growth and expansion of the church, but He used willing human instruments (see Acts 2:14; 3:12; 10:34-48; 11:17; 13:2-4) on whom He bestowed special gifts.

The Life and Work of God's People

What God Expects of His People

What does it mean to be God's people? What does God expect from us? What is our mission? What is the purpose of the church? These are basic questions for us if we are committed to being and doing what God expects of us. They are crucial questions to be answered each time our church develops plans, makes decisions, adopts a budget, or launches a new program or activity.

In essence, the purpose of the church is to carry out the will of Christ in the world, to proclaim and apply His gospel. This involves worship, proclamation and witness, nurture and education, and ministry. Being God's people means fulfilling this purpose. In fulfilling this purpose, God's people are to reach out beyond themselves to communicate the gospel to all people everywhere through evangelism and missions.

Essential Activities for God's People

The activities included in this statement of purpose are essential to the nature of God's people in a church. If any one of them were missing, the nature of the church would be changed.

Worship.—Worship is encountering God in experiences that deepen Christians' faith and strengthen their service and response to mission. The worship of God is foundational to all other church efforts to proclaim and witness, nurture and educate, and minister.

Following the example of Jesus (see Luke 4:16), early churches met regularly for worship. Immediately following Pentecost the church worshiped daily (see Acts 2:46). Places of worship varied: Temple, synagogue, or homes of believers. There is no evidence in the New Testament that the early churches owned property. Subsequently, regular meetings of the Christian fellowship occurred on the first day of the week (see Acts 20:7; 1 Cor. 16:2).

Believers were admonished to attend worship (see Heb. 10:25). Public worship included such ingredients as singing, praying, Scripture reading, preaching, and teaching (see Col. 3:16; 1 Tim. 2:1-2; 4:13). The Lord's Supper was a principal act of worship. Paul gave instructions about order and decorum in worship (1 Cor. 12—14). Finally, the Book of Revelation portrays the triumphant church engaged in worship in heaven (see Rev. 5:9-13; 11:17; 15:3-4). The church cannot be the church apart from the worship of Almighty God.

Proclamation and witness.—All of God's people are responsible for proclaiming the gospel and bearing witness to the saving power of Christ. Jesus came preaching, calling for repentance and obedience to God's kingly rule (see Mark 1:14). One of His first acts was to call out followers who would share this mission (see Mark 1:16-20). He taught His disciples essential truths and sent them out on mission to proclaim the kingdom of God and to give witness to the compassion and power of the Father (see Matt. 10:5-15; Mark 6:7-13; Luke 9:1-6; 10:1-17). After His resurrection He commissioned them to be witnesses of the good news, to make disciples everywhere, and to ground new converts in his teaching (see Luke 24:46-48; Matt. 28:18-20; John 20:21).

God's people are to communicate the gospel not only to persons nearby but also to persons wherever they are, to the uttermost part of the earth (see Acts 1:8) through evangelism and missions. God expects His people to have an outward, missionizing thrust designed to break down barriers that separate persons from God, from society, and from one another. Obeying Jesus' commission includes penetrating new frontiers with the gospel, acting out of a belief that the field is the whole world.

Through response to the Good News proclaimed by God's people, vital Christian discipleship begins with an authentic salvation experience. But making disciples includes more than winning persons to repentance and faith in Christ. Discipleship has corporate relationships and responsibilities, and it finds its fullest meaning within the fellowship of God's people in a church.

The power for proclamation and witness comes from the Holy Spirit (see Acts 1:8; 10:42). The Book of Acts shows the early church empowered and guided by the Spirit as the believers faithfully gave witness to the living Lord and proclaimed God's judgment on sin but His mercy for sinners (see Acts 1:22; 2:4; 3:15; 4:33). A church on mission proclaims redemption for all persons and transforms society.

Nurture and education.—The New Testament leaves no doubt that nurture and education are important to the life and work of God's people in a church. Together, nurture and education include the whole process by which the church prepared persons for the acceptance of Christ and after that guided their development in discipleship toward the goal of Christian maturity. Nurture and education go together like the two sides of a coin. Nurture is the sum of experiences that nourish, influence, and develop individuals within the fellowship of a church. It suggests a loving guardianship. Education involves the more structured means provided for growth in knowledge, wisdom, moral righteousness, and service. Both are concerned with developing competent, fully grown Christians who can themselves share in nurturing and educating others.

The early churches took seriously Jesus' command to make disciples and to teach them (see Matt. 28:20). The disciple is a learner (see Matt. 11:29)—that is the meaning of the word itself, but a disciple is also a doer. Discipleship requires action. Disciples are called upon to share the Master's life and work (see Matt. 20:22-23), to be servants (see John 13:1-20; Mark 10:45) who minister in love and witness with power and joy, corporately and individually (see John 13:34-35). See chapter 6 for additional discussion of discipleship.

The New Testament gives evidence that early churches carefully instructed new converts in the faith, following a simple pattern of teaching (see Acts 2:42; 1 Cor. 15:1-7; 2 Thess. 2:15). New believers were added to church; there was never any question as to whether they would join the fellowship of believers.

Within that fellowship new Christians were expected to grow in grace and knowledge toward full maturity in Christ (see 2 Pet. 3:18; Eph. 4:11-13).

Individuals were responsible for their Christian growth and action (see 2 Tim. 2:15; 2 Pet. 1:5-11), but the church was instructed to help them grow and serve. Church leaders were to feed the flock (see John 21:15-17; 1 Pet. 5:2; Acts 20:28), and the pastor-teacher was to equip the saints for ministry (see Eph. 4:11-13).

Jesus placed a special emphasis on the relationship between learning and faith when He specifically added the dedication of the mind to those elements of the individual to be used in loving God, as given in Deuteronomy 6:4-5, "Thou shalt love the Lord thy God with all thy heart, and with all thy soul, and with all thy mind" (Matt. 22:37).

Church growth in the New Testament is both numerical and spiritual. The church is built up from within through education and nurture, unity in worship, fellowship, and the cultivation and proper use of spiritual gifts (see Acts 2:41-47).

A low level of spiritual development brought forth censure and strong admonitions from church leaders in the New Testament (see 1 Cor. 3:1-4; Heb. 5:12 to 6:3). The transmission of the gospel itself called for the development of faithful witnesses (2 Tim. 2:2).

Through involving non-Christians in educational activities that it provides locally and around the world, a church evangelizes to win the unsaved and then guide them toward Christian maturity. God expects His people to develop toward the goal of Christian maturity and to help one another in this pilgrimage.

Ministry.—Numerous New Testament passages make it clear that God expects His people to minister to the needs of others. The church receives its model for ministry from Jesus Christ, the perfect example of sacrificial, self-giving love. He "went about doing good" (Acts 10:38), ministering to human need, challenging abuses of power, and instructing His followers to give themselves in unselfish and gracious service to others (see Matt. 20:25-28; John 13:15).

The ministry to which Christ calls His followers takes many forms (see Matt. 25:34-40); but it is distinctive because it is done in Christ's name and for His glory, not out of purely humanitarian motives or a desire for praise from others.

Ministry involves practical acts of helping other Christians who are in need. But beyond that, ministry involves the church, individually and collectively, in doing good to all persons (see Gal. 6:10) both through direct efforts and through cooperative efforts with other churches. True ministry in Christ's name calls for positive action reflecting the spirit of Christ, "good works and acts of charity" (Acts 9:36, RSV), not mere words (see Jas. 2:14-17).

A church that follows Jesus' example seeks to minister to the whole person by showing concern for the spiritual, mental, emotional, and physical welfare of both fellow Christians and the unsaved (see Acts 3:6; 6:1-6; 16:16-18; 19:11-12; Rom. 15:25-27).

Acts of ministry to persons outside a church's membership become effective means for evangelistic proclamation and witness by word as well as by example. *Angel Tree*

God's Power for Mission
According to the New Testament, God expects His people to seek maximum moral and spiritual power in their lives and in the body of the church as a whole. Powerless Christians and weak churches indicate the absence of the Holy Spirit, our source of energy. Jesus foresaw his followers engaged in extensive labors and promised the power of the Spirit to help them accomplish their God-given mission (see John 14:12; Acts 1:8). The coming of the Spirit released the church for its task to evangelize the world and undergirded it for effective witnessing (see Acts 2:4). The Book of Acts gives numerous examples of the Holy Spirit's work in the life of the early churches. He directed and empowered the church for its mission

(see Acts 13:2-4; 16:6-10); strengthened God's people for their constant warfare with principalities and powers (see Eph. 6:10-18); and gave a spirit of power, love, and self-control (2 Tim. 1:7). In the face of hostile powers both human and demonic, God's people can do effective work for Christ only if they draw on the power available from the Holy Spirit.

The purpose of the church is to be implemented with a sense of mission according to the calling of God. A church worships, proclaims and witnesses, nurtures and educates, and ministers through the power of the Holy Spirit not only for the benefit of its members and their families but also to reach the greater community—"into all the world" (Mark 16:15).

Organization and Leaders for God's People

Organization in New Testament Churches

New Testament churches started out with no prescribed organizational structure. Generally, organizational patterns took shape in response to developing needs for officers and leaders, structure and policies, and agreement as to purposes and plans. But we must never forget that the churches were more than organizations. They were organisms; they had life. They were expressions of the body of Christ in their communities. This fact set them apart from all merely human institutions.

The absence of a fixed pattern of organization has led modern scholars (depending on their bias) to see in the records traces of a presbyterial, an episcopal, or a congregational form of church government. Baptists have generally felt the congregational pattern to be the most strongly supported in Scripture. Such passages as 1 Corinthians 5:3-5; Galatians 6:1; Acts 6:2-4; Acts 13:1-3; and Acts 15:22-35 give evidence that the members participated in the governing process of the church. In some instances the business affairs of the total body seem to have been handled by the apostles and elders (see Acts 15:2,6).

The New Testament contains no statements of policy in the modern sense, but it does give evidence of autonomous congregations managing their own affairs, at times choosing to cooperate with other churches but subject only to the lordship of Christ. As a priestly community (see 1 Pet. 2:4-10) possessing a diversity of gifts for ministry (see Rom. 12:4-6; 1 Cor. 12; Eph. 4:1-16), a church is like a democratic society in which all members participate and bear responsibility. In another sense the church is a theocratic society, for it exists under divine rule.

From a review of the New Testament, we can identify certain principles of church organization.

• Each church is an autonomous spiritual body under the leadership of Christ.

• All members have equal rights and privileges in the church. (This principle is rooted in the fundamental Christian doctrine of the priesthood of all believers.)

• Each member ought to be meaningfully involved in the functioning of the church (see Rom. 12:4-8; 1 Cor. 12).

• Organization must serve the purposes of the church.

• Organization should be suited to needs and situations as they develop.

• Churches are interdependent with other churches for mutual support and effort.

In the absence of specific instructions about organization, churches should be open to flexibility and innovation in organizational patterns, though adhering to New Testament principles. Because the Spirit of God is at work within the churches, He may lead them to create new structures to meet developing needs. Each congregation of God's people is free to determine its pattern of organization in keeping with a Bible-based and Spirit-guided understanding of its mission.

Leaders for God's People

The principle of Christian leadership is grounded in the purposes of God for the church (see 1 Cor. 12:28; Eph. 4:11). Leadership opportunities come to the entire body of believers as they minister according to their gifts. A diversity of gifts is needed to make the church fully a functioning body. The New Testament discusses two types of leaders in local churches: pastors (elders or overseers) and deacons.

Pastor.—The word *pastor* (*poimen*, shepherd) fittingly describes the shepherding function which pastors are expected to perform. The terms *elder* (*presbyteros,* older man) and *overseer* (*episcopos,* sometimes translated "bishop") seem to refer to the same church officer, for they are used interchangeably. Baptists have generally preferred the term *pastor* that emphasizes a shepherd's care of the flock of God, but we expect a pastor to be mature (not a novice) and to fulfill some administrative duties. Probably the phrase "pastors and teachers" (Eph. 4:11) refers to one office. If so, the shepherd is ideally a "pastor-teacher" (see 1 Tim. 3:2).[6]

Some New Testament churches apparently had not one but several pastors. This was true of the church at Jerusalem (see Acts 11:30; 15:2,4,6,22-23; 16:4; 21:18), the church at Ephesus (see Acts 20:17,28), and possibly elsewhere (see Acts 14:23). This plurality of elders may have been required to minister to the scattered congregations that make up the church in these cities.

Deacons.—The other major office in the New Testament churches was that of deacon. Used only five times in the New Testament (Phil. 1:1; 1 Tim. 3:8,10,12-13), the word *deacon* (*diakonos,* "servant, minister") refers to an important office to be filled by persons possessing high moral qualities (1 Tim. 3:8-13). They are ministers and must be able to perform such ministries as the church may require.

The lives of both pastors (overseers, elders) and deacons must be exemplary. Their soundness and maturity in the faith and their dependence on the Holy Spirit must be well attested (see 1 Tim. 3:1-13; Titus 1:6-9). The Scriptures put heavy emphasis on the moral and spiritual qualifications of leaders but say little about specific duties.

Church leaders evidently were chosen by the congregation in a democratic fashion. In the selection of the seven (see Acts 6:1-6), the apostles asked the congregation to state their preferences and "they chose" Stephen and six others. The choice of leaders for other specific assignments was also made in a democratic, congregational manner (see Acts 15:22; 1 Cor. 16:3).

Out of a review of practices in New Testament churches, some abiding principles regarding church leaders may be stated:

• Churches act responsibly when they adhere to biblical standards in the selection of leaders.

• The entire congregation must be involved in this process of selection.

• The New Testament's qualifications for pastors and deacons must be taken seriously.

Relationships of God's People

Each church exists in a network of relationships. Leaders and members need to be fully aware of these relationships and to maintain them in ways that will help achieve the church's mission.

Relationships Within a Church

Church members have individual functions; but they are mutually dependent, each needing the others. A church best fulfills its mission and ministry when there is a division of labor in which all members exercise their gifts and do their share of the work (see Rom. 12:4-12; 1 Cor. 12; Eph. 4:11-16). The example and spirit of Jesus and the love He commanded set a pattern for relationships within a church (see John 13:1-15). The New Testament teaches mutual respect among members, mutual helpfulness, mutual forbearance, joint efforts for harmony, and sincere forgiveness (see 1 Cor. 12:31 to 14:1; Eph. 4:1-3; Col. 3:12-13; 1 Thess. 5:12-15; 1 Pet. 3:8-9). Relationships within a church can be disrupted by immaturities, selfishness, and misguided zeal, as illustrated by the Corinthian church. But God's people are to "be subject to one another out of reverence for Christ" (Eph. 5:21, RSV).

Relationships with Other Churches

The New Testament provides examples of relationships with other churches.

The threat of a common problem brought representatives of churches together for discussion and action (see Acts 15) resulting in a compromise statement which was sent out to the churches.

Cooperation among churches was sometimes a response to human need, as in the case of the special offering which the Gentile churches raised for the relief of the poor in Jerusalem (see Rom. 15:15-16; Acts 24:17; 2 Cor. 8—9).

Entertaining visiting preachers and members was another way

New Testament churches jointly shared responsibilities (see 3 John 5-6; Rom. 12:13; Heb. 13:2; Titus 3:13). This was done to meet a need and because Christian love encouraged hospitality. Itinerant churchmen both received and bestowed blessings when admitted to a household.

There is no New Testament evidence that relating to other churches caused a congregation to lose its independence or autonomy or that any church or combination of churches imposed regulations on other congregations. Mutual support and cooperation grew out of the churches' common relationship to Jesus Christ.

Two guiding principles characterized relationships with other churches in New Testament times: (1) mutual respect and brotherly love, and (2) voluntariness and freedom coupled with responsibility.

Relationships with Society

To be an effective force in society, God's people must understand the relationship of the church to society. The New Testament church was in tension with the "world" (society in alienation from God, often radically opposed to Him). The Lord said that His people are "not of the world" but are to be in the world, protected from the evil one by the Holy Spirit (John 17:14). The contrasts between the Christian community and the world are sharply drawn (see Eph. 2:1-13), and believers are enjoined neither to love the world (see 1 John 2:15-17) nor to conform to its standards and life-styles (see Rom. 12:2). But God's people live within the world, not in monastic withdrawal from society. Jesus described His followers as salt and light (see Matt. 5:13-14), a redemptive society touching the life of the world.

Seeking to bring all persons into a saving relationship with Jesus Christ is the major responsibility of a church to the world about it. The Holy Spirit repeatedly led New Testament churches to make a definite outreach for souls in the name of the Lord (see Acts 13:1-3; 14:26-27; Phil. 4:10-18; 3 John 5-8).

In addition to personal evangelism, God's people must take a positive stand for righteousness and work earnestly to bring about mutual respect, brotherhood, justice, and peace in all relationships of people, races, and nations.

Relationships with the State

Relationships between church and state are becoming increasinging complex in our day, but the New Testament provides some guidance for churches in these relationships. Both church and state have been instituted by God and are answerable to Him (see Rom. 13:1). Each is distinct in purpose and function, as implied in Jesus' saying, "Render to Caesar the things that are Caesar's, and to God the things that are God's" (Mark 12:17; see Matt. 22:21; Luke 20:25). The principle here is that persons who benefit from government owe a proportionate share of the cost of such benefits. Church and state are to remain separate but are to be in proper relationship with each other under God.

The New Testament teaches that Christians should pray for those in authority and obey them when no violation of conscience is involved.

✎ ::

Pause and Do: *Personal Learning Activity 1*
1. Write a brief definition of the church in your own words. Make it as short as possible to cover the subject.
2. Give a summary statement of the mission (or purpose) of the church.
3. Name four essential activities for God's people in a church. Is your church doing all of these activities equally well? If not, which one(s) need(s) strengthening?

::

1"Missions Scope" (A paper prepared by the Missions Education Council, Southern Baptist Convention, n.d.), p. 2.

2Frank Stagg, *New Testament Theology* (Nashville: Broadman Press, 1962), p. 191.

3From the Revised Standard Version of the Bible, copyrighted 1946, 1952, © 1971, 1973. Subsequent quotations are marked RSV.

4*The Baptist Faith and Message: a Statement Adopted by the Southern Baptist Convention* (Nashville: Sunday School Board of the Southern Baptist Convention, 1963), pp. 12-13.

5See "Report of the Missions Challenge Committee to the Southern Baptist Convention," *1976 SBC Annual,* pp. 53-55.

6For references to elders in the New Testament, see Acts 11:30; 14:23;

15:2,4,6,22-23; 16:4; 20:17; 21:18; 1 Timothy 5:17,19; Titus 1:5; James 5:14; 1 Peter 5:1. For references to bishops, see Philippians 1:1; 1 Timothy 3:1-2; Titus 1:7; 1 Peter 5:2. For references to pastors, see Acts 20:28; Ephesians 4:11; 1 Peter 5:2.

CHAPTER 2

Understanding the Needs of Persons

What does understanding the needs of persons have to do with the work of your church? Take a few moments to think through the answer to this question as preparation for studying this chapter.

Our study of biblical material about New Testament churches refreshes our awareness that God expects His people to focus their efforts on bringing persons to salvation and helping them to grow and serve. God's people are to be concerned about the needs of both saved and unsaved persons, those like us and those who are different—all persons everywhere. If God's people are to enter new frontiers with the gospel as He expects, our efforts to minister to human needs must take us beyond the church building and the membership of the church family. A full understanding of human needs is essential for a church that wants to be effective in witnessing to the lost and ministering to specific needs of persons it can reach. Such understanding is foundational in setting a church's priorities and developing its program. God's people must strive to see the needs of persons as He sees them and respond to them according to His priorities.

Needs are the mainsprings of human behavior. A *need* may be defined as "a drive, motive, urge, desire, or instinct that causes persons to act as they do." A need may be a "push" caused by a lack or deficit, or it may be a "pull" caused by a goal or desire. Needs are intensely personal. They may not be observable or even consciously known to the person. The strength of needs to shape behavior varies greatly according to the person's environment, cultural background, and ability to respond. Although scientists have contributed much to our understanding of the needs of persons, the insights derived from the Bible are essential for God's people to understand the true nature of persons and to respond to their deepest needs.

The Spiritual Nature and Needs of Persons

Created by God in His Image

Many Scripture passages make it clear that the creation of a person, a human being made in His own likeness, was the peak of God's creative activity (see Ps. 8:3–8). At each stage of creation, God said that it was good; but when He created man and woman, He went beyond such an expression. He gave them stewardship over all creation.

Each person is a creation of God and bears the image of God (see Gen. 1:27). Made in God's moral and spiritual likeness, each individual possesses reason, will power, freedom of choice, and a capacity for personal fellowship with the Creator. The fact that a person shares God's nature gives him or her a dignity and value above all other creatures. God has bestowed His love upon mankind, and the true purpose of every person is to honor and glorify God. Relationship to God's image is seen in the emotional, volitional and rational, and social chacteristics of persons and in their potential.

Emotional beings.—As emotional beings, persons are capable of feeling. This ability gives them the capacity to love, without which a person could not relate meaningfully to self, to others, or to God. God is love; He is a feeling God. To respond to Him, persons made in His image are also feeling beings.

Volitional and rational capacity.—Persons are capable of exercising will and reason. This capacity transcends the physical. It provides the ability to project meaning.

Social nature.—The social nature of persons gives them the ability to relate meaningfully to other God-created persons as social beings to have fellowship with one another.

Persons of potential.—Persons created in the image of God have within them the potential to be a part of God's continuing creation in the world. That potential is increased in those who have been re-created into the image of Christ. Persons who are open to the leadership of God's Spirit and the resurrection power made available through Jesus Christ will realize continuing growth toward their full potential.

More than an Earthly Creature

Made for fellowship with God (see Gen. 5:24), each person is more than a creature of earth. There is eternity in the human heart. Jesus "abolished death and brought life and immortality to light through the gospel" (2 Tim. 1:10, RSV). He said, "I am the resurrection, and the life: he that believeth in me, though he were dead, yet shall he live: and whosoever liveth and believeth in me shall never die" (John 11:25–26).

Uniquely Gifted

God is the Creator not just of humankind as a species but of every individual person. He has created every person as an original being with definite and unique gifts. The followers of Christ have been given gifts for the "equipping of the saints . . . to the building up of the body of Christ" (Eph. 4:12, NASB).[1] A gift is a concrete and personal realization of grace in the life of the believer. Through such gifts persons discover the essence and purpose of their lives, and God continues His creative work.

Valued by God

Every human being is of great value in God's sight and must not be abused or exploited (see Matt. 18:10-14). Each person is one "for whom Christ died" (1 Cor. 8:11). God makes no artificial distinctions between persons, and in Christ all human barriers between individuals are obliterated (see Acts 10:34; 15:8-9; Gal. 3:28; Col. 3:11). Because God places persons in such high esteem, it follows that He expects His children to hold themselves in the highest esteem and to treat one another as persons of great worth (Lev. 19:18; Matt. 22:39). The supreme value of persons is a vital basic concept in self-understanding.

Capable of Relationship with Him

Created in the image of God, a person can enter into personal relationship with Him. No human mediator is needed to bring an individual into the divine presence. Jesus Christ, who is both God and man, is the true Mediator who brings God and mankind together (see 1 Tim. 2:5; Heb. 10:19-22). Christ also strengthens in persons the will to obey God. Persons have been created for obedience, and their true security and purpose are realized in faithful adherence to God's intention.

Endowed with Freedom of Choice

Adam and Eve were given the freedom to choose how they would live, but they had a responsibility to obey God. Freedom means that in the human personality God did not make a puppet on a string but an individual with the freedom of self-determination.

God gave persons the freedom to choose good or evil. Without it a person's worship of God would be worthless. Love and adoration are meaningless if they do not arise out of free will. All meaningful relationships are built on the premise of mutual freedom and responsibility.

Though freedom presents tremendous opportunity, it carries with it considerable risk and responsibility for the consequences of one's choices. Jesus grieved over the city of Jerusalem, but He did not take responsibility for the people's behavior.

Marred by Sin

The biblical picture of persons is not complete without exploring how men and women have responded to their freedom. By choosing disobedience, Adam and Eve disrupted their special fellowship with God which was based on a relationship of both freedom and obedience. The account in Genesis 3 of their willful plunge into sin depicts human rebellion against God and its shattering effect on human life. They failed to live up to the full potential that God had placed in them. From that experience until the present, individuals have continued to use their freedom to disobey, causing a broken relationship between themselves and God. "Our freedom," says William Hendricks, "has produced evil which causes both us and God to suffer."[2]

The New Testament amply notes the sinfulness of human nature, the presence of satanic forces in human affairs, and the helplessness of persons to save themselves. Sin in general is missing the mark, falling short of God's intention for persons. The Hebrew understanding of sin as rebellion and falling short is echoed in the New Testament (see 1 John 5:17; Rom. 3:23). Biblical writers used a variety of terms to describe sin: transgression or rebellion; iniquity or crooked, perverted conduct; lying and deceit; godlessness; lawlessness; lustfulness; wickedness or depravity; and unbelief, which is the essence of sin.

In various ways a person seeks to handle the contradiction at the center of his or her being—denying guilt, seeking to justify conduct, revising views of God, or altering the scale of values. But like the guilty pair in Eden, one can never escape the judgment of God. Ultimately, His holiness asserts itself and takes issue with our wickedness.

Though it is true that God is love and takes no delight in the death of the wicked, it is equally true that He takes no delight in the wickedness of their lives. The biblical view of God includes His judgment upon sin (see Luke 13:3,5; John 3:16,36; Acts 17:30-31). Sin causes estrangement from the God who created us for fellowship with Him. In strong language the New Testament declares that unregenerate persons are outside God's kingdom and are in danger of death or eternal separation from God. There is no basis in the Bible for an easygoing, permissive view of mankind's waywardness and alienation from God.

Because human beings are influenced by both God and Satan, they are not always predictable. There is a continuing struggle within each person between the intention of God's creation and the tug to disobey, to be less than God meant him or her to be.

Persons marred by sin are self-centered. Each is turned inward and generally gives first priority to selfish needs and desires. It becomes easy to manipulate persons to one's own advantage. Self-sacrifice is difficult.

Self-centeredness is not altogether negative. Some degree of it may simply be self-esteem, a sense of self-worth that enables a person to celebrate his or her gifts and to relate meaningfully to others. The Scriptures say, "Love your neighbor as yourself" (Matt. 19:19, RSV). Self-love, then, is a model for loving others. Only when a person carries that sense of self-worth to excess does it become detrimental.

Redeemed by Love

God's initiative.—Despite the human guilt of sin, God took the initiative to search out Adam and Eve after they had sinned. This searching love has continued to be God's response to the rebellion of his sons and daughters. Because sin separated mankind from the holy God, He found it necessary to deal with transgression. Salvation was provided through His Son, Jesus Christ; and rescue was effected from our moral and spiritual ruin (see Rom. 5:6-11; 2 Cor. 5:14-21). The means of rescue was provided by Christ's death on the cross. Ultimate victory over sin was sealed and guaranteed by His resurrection. New life was provided to every person who would accept it (see Phil. 3:10-11). "God offered him, so that by his death he should become the means by which people's sins are forgiven through their faith in him" (Rom. 3:25, GNB).[3]

Human response required.—Human response to God's initiative is necessary to receive new life in Christ. Because of God's great love for all persons, He has made a way for each returning person to be forgiven and restored to the fellowship that was marred by sin. But God does not force His gifts on anyone. Each person is free to accept or reject His redeeming, fellowship-restoring love. Guilty and separated from God, a person needs forgiveness and reconciliation with the Creator but cannot bridge the gap or wrench free from sin (see Job 9:2; Isa. 64:6; Jer. 17:9-10). God's provision for dealing with sin and restoring fellowship has given each person the capacity to rise above self-centeredness and recapture in his or her personality the Godlike traits of love and forgiveness.

Eternal destiny rests with a person's response to God's love. Acceptance of God's redemption through Christ brings a definite and forever experience of salvation. This is the good news that all people must hear (see Rom. 10:14-17), and proclamation of this truth is the church's essential mission in every generation. The fact that sinful persons can and do respond to God's love gives meaning and purpose to the work of the church.

Other Basic Needs of Persons

In addition to the spiritual needs of persons to which churches must give priority attention, all persons have certain other basic needs. These needs may be classified into five categories: physiological needs, safety needs, social needs, esteem needs, and growth needs.[4] These needs must also be considered in shaping the program of a church.

Physiological Needs

Physiological needs are those innate, biogenic drives that stimulate a person to preserve life and health. They are basic to human development. Included in these needs are hunger and thirst, rest and sleep, elimination, respiration, sexual gratification, bodily exercise, comfortable temperature, and pain avoidance. The relative significance of each of these needs to the individual may be conditioned by culture and individual values.

Many of these physiological needs are generally satisfied away from the church building. However, such conveniences as meals, heating and air conditioning, rest rooms, water fountains, and facilities for Christian recreation and exercise are some of the ways congregations acknowledge the motivational strength of these needs.

Satisfaction of some physiological needs may be linked with the satisfaction of other needs. For example, when persons are satisfying the need for food at a church meal, they may also be satisfying the social need for fellowship (belonging).

In their efforts to share the gospel of Christ, however, God's people need to remember that a person whose physiological needs are not being met adequately is less likely to respond to incentives based on higher needs. A starving man has little immediate concern for self-esteem.

Safety Needs

Safety needs include the needs for security; stability; dependence; protection; freedom from fear, anxiety, and chaos; structure; order; law; limits; and strength in the protector. These needs generally emerge when a person's physiological needs are relatively well met.

You can readily see that this category of needs has many implications for the work of a church. For example, safety needs play a significant role in a person's decision to become a Christian. The Holy Spirit often works through the felt need for eternal security to bring a person to repentance and faith. The needs for structure, order, limits, and a strong protector are involved in becoming a disciple of Christ.

A person's response to change and new information may be strongly influenced by the need for security, stability, familiar structure, and order. For example, the reluctance of some adults to change Bible study classes as they age may be understood as their way of resisting a threat to their needs for stability, structure, and order. Wise church leaders will seek to reduce the threat of instability when proposing changes.

Social Needs

Social needs include the need to love and be loved, to interact with others, to feel accepted, and to belong. Persons are social beings, created by God to be in a relationship of love and fellowship with Him and with others.

Giving affection is also a significant social need. For Christians, giving is an important way to express their Christian faith. Our Lord said, "Love one another; as I have loved you" (John 13:34). Paul stated, "Love one another warmly as Christian brothers" (Rom. 12:10, GNB).

A church relates meaningfully to these needs because it is a fellowship of believers united in Christ. The small-group activities of a church meet the fellowship needs of many persons. A church's efforts to witness and minister provide opportunities for expressions of love.

The need for love and acceptance is universal. Until a person has experienced some fulfillment of these needs, he cannot achieve the potential that God has placed in him.

Esteem Needs

Esteem is a higher order of need than social, safety, and physical well-being. *Esteem* means "high regard." All persons need a stable, firmly based, usually high evaluation of themselves for self-esteem and for esteem from others.

Self-esteem includes needs such as the desire for confidence, competence, mastery, adequacy, achievement, independence, and freedom.—A person's self-image is built on self-esteem and is often a controlling factor in happiness and achievement. It appears that when persons reach their preconceived level of status or prestige, the strength of this need tends to decline and become a matter of maintenance rather than further advancement. For example, a person may be highly motivated until he reaches his perceived high-water mark in Christian development but then cease to grow because he has satisfied his self-image.

On the other hand, many persons are frustrated in their mid-years because they have reached all of their goals (education, family, etc.) but have not achieved as much as they had hoped (often called mid-career crisis). They find themselves having to shift emotionally from tangible goals to quality-of-life goals, and the transition is often not easy.

Esteem from others includes the needs for prestige, recognition, acceptance, attention, status, reputation, and appreciation.—Each of us wants and needs to be appreciated by others. A person's self-esteem is built largely on feedback received from others. There is a real danger, however, in basing one's self-esteem totally on such feedback because it often stems from the other person's needs and includes many biases. Self-esteem is more stable and healthy when it is based on deserved respect from others.

The meeting of esteem needs is important in church life. Because the church and Christian leaders are important in the life of a Christian, the affirmation or rejection a person receives from them is highly significant to his self-esteem. Rejection by a minister for some persons may feel like rejection by God. Ministers, therefore, have the power to bless or to curse.

Growth Needs

Within each person is the need to become all he or she can become. Sometimes referred to as "self-actualization," this need emerges only after a reasonable satisfaction of social and esteem needs.

Actions in pursuit of a person's growth needs appear to differ from those in other need areas. Physiological, safety, social, and esteem needs appear to operate in a cycle which begins with a deficit or disequilibrium that causes the person to alter behavior as necessary to satisfy the deficit. Growth actions, however, appear to stem not from a deficit but from a need to achieve, to become, and to give or pass on something of oneself to others. Some persons have a high need for achievement and tend to stretch themselves to become all their potential will allow.

Among Christians the term "being on mission" expresses well the concept of stretching to become all that God has given the capacity to become and of directing that capacity toward the achievement of goals related to His purposes. Paul was reflecting growth needs when he said, "I press toward the mark for the prize of the high calling of God in Christ Jesus" (Phil. 3:14). As discussed in chapter 1, God expects His people to grow and to help others grow to the full potential He has given them in creation and through re-creation in Christ.

Developmental Needs of Persons

Developmental needs relate to the various stages of development from infancy through adulthood, needs and learning tasks which come to all of us.

Churches recognize these needs when they group persons for learning and fellowship into classes or groups for preschoolers, children, youth, and adults—young, middle-aged, and senior—and when they provide facilities, equipment, materials, and activities suited to the age group. Because these needs are dealt with at length in a variety of high quality materials available to leaders who work with age divisions, they will not be summarized here.[5] As an indication of concern for developmental needs, a church should provide adequate training for its age-group teachers and leaders.

Crisis Needs of Persons

Persons also experience crisis needs which grow out of their life situations and may be felt with devastating impact because their timing usually cannot be anticipated. A *crisis* is "an emotionally significant event or radical change of status in a person's life."

Crisis needs arise out of two broad categories, personal crises and relational crises. A brief listing of the experiences that fall in each category will suffice to show the scope of a church's oportunity for ministry and witness in these experiences.

Personal Crises

Health.—Most persons experience mental, emotional, physical, or spiritual illness at some time in their lives. Positive crises such as childbirth can also be experienced.

Financial problems.—These may come from poor money management, inflation, job layoff, unwise investments, unforeseen emergencies, and excess credit buying. A sudden windfall is also a crisis.

Vocational crises.—Loss of job, demotion, promotion, move, and stalemate are some examples.

Material loss.—Fires, tornadoes, floods, and theft are the most frequent causes of material loss.

Relational Crises

Family.—Divorce, delinquency, desertion, marital problems, and drug abuse are indications of relational problems within the family.

Church.—Tensions and disgreements relating to rapid church growth, church programs, discipline, policies, procedures, and other areas may create crises in the fellowship of the church. A need may also exist for establishing previously nonexistent relationships or deepening superficial ones.

Community.—Crises may come in relationships in the school; between neighbors; or in clubs, associations, or other groups. Blight, poverty, integration, misunderstandings, and other types of disputes may cause relationships to be broken or marred. For many students and young adults the large issues of draft and war and peace become matters of critical concern.

Vocations.—Crises in the relationship between the individual and his or her supervisor, peers, or subordinates may exist. Policy sometimes brings crisis, especially when an individual's convictions are being compromised.

Death.—Loss of a mate, relative, or friend provokes crisis. Suicide within a family or church presents a unique, intense crisis.

Persons who are confronted with a crisis situation may suffer physically or experience disillusionment regarding life, religion, and personal relationships. The person in crisis may need practical help such as food, care for children, help with everyday chores, financial advice, or assistance with business and legal matters. The need may be for prayer support, a listening ear, or help in understanding and accepting their condition. Some may need referral to professional help. Such crisis experiences give God's people opportunities to witness and minister to others and to demonstrate their faith as they cope with their own crises.

Contextual Factors That Influence the Needs of Persons

Increasingly important in contemporary society are contextual factors that significantly influence the experience of the various needs of persons. Contextual factors are conditions in a person's life situation or background that influence his or her experiences. Such contextual factors should be given careful study by a church as it shapes its evangelistic and missions outreach. Failure to consider them may cause the church to attempt inappropriate and ineffective responses to the needs that have been identified. Here is an overview of some of the more significant contextual factors.

Geographic
A church must be sensitive to its own geographical influences. Churches sometimes do not give sufficient consideration to more subtle geographic influences in attempting to meet the needs of persons within their reach.

Racial/Ethnic/Cultural
Factors of race, national origin, and culture strongly influence a person's orientation for education and worship. Culture reflects the network of influences that shape the behavior and values which give meaning to life's experiences.

Race and ethnicity create a context of deep-rooted influences that precondition reaction to and acceptance of the church. Language and thought patterns are conditioned by culture and ethnicity. Such patterns often persist long after a person is otherwise socially adjusted to his present life situation. God's people called Southern Baptists need to make adequate provision for these influences in our church programs.

Educational
The nature and extent of a person's education are influenced by his or her situation in life. This education and the value placed on it likewise influence a person's response to society and the church.

Many of the needs and views of young adults in colleges are unlike those of their parents or other young adults. Persons involved in higher education expect programs and services tailored to their particular life situation related to the academic community. This calls for a specialized ministry by the church.

Religious/Philosophical
In a pluralistic society many divergent religious and philosophical systems attempt to order and give meaning to existence. Life under the influence of any religious, political, or philosophical system establishes a predisposition toward understandings of humankind and the world that are not easily changed. Witness, ministry, and mission outreach must be sensitive to this type of faith commitment if the gospel is effectively to encounter these new frontiers.

Socioeconomic
Social class and economic condition influence receptivity and response to the gospel. In all of its work, a church must consciously seek to approach persons on the basis of their expectations and ability to respond as conditioned by their social and economic situation.

Life-style
Some of the influences already described lead persons to life-styles associated with affluence, poverty, geography, and religious persuasion. Others have submitted themselves to subcultural and countercultural influences that shape their perceptions and responses. Finally, the effort to fulfill the ascending needs of social acceptance and self-esteem has led some persons to establish variant or aberrant life-styles that must be considered by any church as it reaches out.

Obeying Jesus' commission to proclaim the good news calls the church to overcome all boundaries in order to penetrate new frontiers with the gospel. In order to gain a hearing for this gospel, the church will have to sensitize itself to the contextually influenced needs of the hearer.

Think back over the needs that have been described in this chapter and decide whether you agree with these statements: (1) In shaping and carrying on a church's programs, church leaders and members must be aware of and responsive to the real needs of the persons they are trying to bring to salvation and growth in Christ. (2) In considering how to meet the needs of persons, the distinctive dimension for churches is the impact of the biblical view of persons with its emphasis on their spiritual nature and needs. This does not mean that churches should not have concern for the whole person. It does mean that commitment to the biblical view of persons distinguishes church activities from those of secular institutions and organizations.

✎ ::

Pause and Do: *Personal Learning Activity 2*
    1. What distinguishes a church's efforts to meet human needs from the efforts of secular organizations?
    2. List two ways your church is demonstrating to persons outside the membership that you are sensitive to their needs and want to lead them into a life-transforming relationship with Christ.
    3. Describe two or three specific ways your church (you) could use information about the needs of persons to be more effective in witness and ministry.

::⊜

---

[1]From the *New American Standard Bible.* Copyright © The Lockman Foundation, 1960, 1962, 1963, 1968, 1971, 1972, 1973, 1975, 1977. Used by permission.

[2]William L. Hendricks, *The Doctrine of Man* (Nashville: Convention Press, 1977), pp. 47-48.

[3]This quotation is from the *Good News Bible,* the Bible in Today's English Version. Old Testament: Copyright © American Bible Society 1976; New Testament: Copyright © American Bible Society 1966, 1971, 1976. Used by permission. Subsequent quotations are marked GNB.

[4]Material in this section on "Other Basic Needs" is adapted from Reginald M. McDonough, comp., *A Church on Mission* (Nashville: Convention Press, 1980), pp. 32-35.

[5]For example, see the Church Study Course books: Lucien E. Coleman, Jr., *Understanding Today's Adults* (Nashville: Convention Press, 1982); Daniel O. Aleshire, *Understanding Today's Youth* (Nashville: Convention Press, 1982); Max B. Price, *Understanding Today's Children* (Nashville: Convention Press, 1982); and C. Sybil Waldrop, *Understanding Today's Preschoolers* (Nashville: Convention Press, 1982).

CHAPTER 3

Turning Concern Into Purposeful Action

For God's people to know what the Bible says about a church and to know about all sorts of human needs, especially spiritual needs, is not enough. It is not enough even to feel concern about being on mission with God and about the needs of persons. Knowledge must inform concern; concern must be turned into Spirit-guided action.

The title of this book, *Being God's People,* is not meant to communicate a static state of being, but rather a dynamic, active response to God's call to share in His life and His mission. Being God's people is more than a relationship; it is participation in His redemptive plan not only as recipients but also as carriers of the good news to as many lost persons as we can reach individually and as churches.

Here is where the people of the old covenant missed the mark. They wanted to enjoy the benefits of the relationship, the special position of being God's people; but they did not fulfill the responsibility of reaching out to bring others to God. They wanted to accept God's covenant "for me, my wife, my children, my relatives, and others like me" and forget the others God was seeking. Before we think too harshly of them and marvel at how they could act that way, let's ask yourselves: "How many of our new church members last year were new converts other than members of church families? How many of those new converts were from a socioeconomic or ethnic background different from that of most of our members? What has been *my* track record in reaching out to witness and minister to unbelievers?"

What Are Your Intentions as God's People, a Church?

Building on biblical teachings about the church and its mission and considering the needs of persons, God's people in a church will find value in stating what they intend to accomplish as a church. Of course, such statements should reflect the biblical teachings about what a church is to be and to do; but they can also be tailored to fit the particular set of opportunities and resources the Lord has given each church in its situation.

What does your church intend to be and to do? The answer to that question will describe the aspirations of your church, its intentions. An intention is what a person or group purposes to accomplish or attain—what a church hopes to become or achieve. In thinking of church life, Southern Baptists have found it helpful to think of intentions in two broad categories—basic intentions and dated intentions.

Basic intentions are what a church desires to be and to achieve on a continuing basis, growing out of and in harmony with its biblical nature and purpose. Statements of basic intentions describe a church's most fundamental aspirations.

Dated intentions are specific, desired outcomes that a church plans to achieve within a definite time period, such as a year or a five-year planning period, within the scope of its basic intentions.

Such intentions are commonly expressed in strategies and/or goals for which detailed, dated action plans are developed.

The remainder of this chapter deals with the kinds of basic intentions statements a church can use to give focus and order to its work.

Basic Intentions

Can you imagine what your church would be like if there were no definite programs of work? No leaders called or elected to be responsible for specific areas of work the church wants to accomplish? Clear statements of basic intentions provide the way for a church to make the most effective use of all the resources the Lord entrusts to it for being on bold mission with Him.

Reasons for Having Clearly Stated Basic Intentions

Several benefits can be gained from having clearly stated basic intentions. Here are three of the most significant.

Integration of a church's program and people.—Statements of basic intentions, when developed by all persons responsible for their achievement, provide the means for linking the ideals and purposes of persons or groups of persons so that all relate meaningfully to the ideals and purposes of the entire church and its work.

Motivation of leaders and members.—People of the congregation are more willing to become involved in the work of the church when they find their intentions are identified with the basic intentions of the church. They are more likely to turn their intentions into actions.

Evaluation and use of resources.—Statements of basic intentions are useful as criteria for evaluation, thereby providing a more effective approach to administration. They provide the best means a church has for monitoring its use of all its resources in order to attain maximum intended results.

Basic Intentions—Three Levels

The complexity of modern life and of church activity and the need for an adequate control system require a series of stated basic intentions, beginning with a summary statement of a church's reason for being and progressing through a series of increasingly more specific statements. Three levels of basic intention statements have been found helpful in clarifying a church's intentions—church mission, church functions, and church tasks.

The Mission of a Church

A statement of a church's mission gives a brief but comprehensive summary description of a church's reason for being, the basic purpose for which it exists, as based on biblical teachings. A mission statement becomes the spring from which all other church intentions statements flow. It gives direction to all succeeding statements of intention, all of which must be within its scope.

An Example of a Church Mission Statement

The mission of a church is to be a redemptive body in Christ through the power of the Holy Spirit, committed to worship, to proclaim and witness, to nurture and educate, and to minister in order to grow toward Christian maturity and to show to all the world what God has done, is doing, and promises to do in Jesus Christ, to the end that God's purposes may be achieved. (See chapter 1 for a full discussion of material on which this statement is based.)

The Functions of a Church

Church functions are statements of basic intentions that should lead a church to do its work in ways consistent with its nature and mission. They indicate essential areas of work in which actions are performed on a continuing basis and without which the basic nature of the church would be altered. They may also be thought of as statements of functional objectives.

To be is to function. What a person, organism, or organization does is normally the best clue to its nature. A church worships, proclaims and witnesses, nurtures and educates, and ministers.

These functions are performed by the church as a congregation, by large or small groups of members, and by individual members within their sphere of relationships. Churches can reach beyond their own capabilities and local situation by combining their resources with those of other churches, following the New Testament pattern of voluntary, Spirit-led cooperation.

These functions may occur in the church facilities, in the community, in the home, and wherever individual church members—the people of God—can go or communicate through direct and representative efforts.

The following are church functions stated as intentions. The definition and description of each function are brief summary statements based on the corresponding section under the heading "Essential Activities for God's People" in chapter 1.

Our intention is to worship.—Worship means "encountering God in experiences that deepen a Christian's faith and strengthen a Christian's service." In worship there is a response to God's presence in adoration and praise, in confession of sin and repentance, and in thanksgiving and service.

Worship is encountering God in spirit and in truth. This may be done in public or in private; individually or in groups; in the church building, the home, or other locations; in structured services and in informal activities; and through ministry and witness activities in which God's presence is strongly felt.

Our intention is to proclaim and witness.—This function involves communicating the message of God's work of grace in Christ which has as its central purpose bringing all persons to confess Jesus as Lord and accept Him as Savior.

Through proclamation and witness believers use all available means to communicate the message of Christ. Proclamation emphasizes verbal presentation of the gospel to others, both unbelievers and believers, often in structured settings. Witnessing emphasizes the day-to-day, informal sharing of the gospel with others through the words, deeds, and life-style of God's people. Proclamation and witness include both what a church and its members do directly and what they do in cooperation with other churches in representative efforts through the association, state convention, and Southern Baptist Convention to communicate the gospel to the uttermost part of the earth.

Our intention is to nurture and educate.—This function involves guiding persons in their progressive development toward Christian maturity. It includes teaching, training, fellowship, and personal involvement designed to help a church and individuals grow toward a mature Christian faith and life. It begins prior to conversion and extends throughout life.

Nurture is the sum of experiences that nourish, influence, and develop individuals within the fellowship of the church. Education involves the more structured means provided for growth in knowledge, wisdom, righteousness, and service. Guiding persons in their development involves both what a church does directly and what it does in cooperation with other churches.

Our intention is to minister.—The verb *minister* means meeting crucial spiritual and physical needs in the spirit of Christ, thus recognizing that a church must have concern for the whole person. Notice the emphasis on concern for the whole person. Though a church is greatly concerned about meeting the basic spiritual needs of persons, our Lord taught us also to demonstrate concern for other human needs. This church function includes the service a church and its members perform both directly and in cooperation with other churches for the lost, the estranged, the destitute, the deprived, and the suffering within its own membership, in its community, and throughout the world.

As you think about these intentions called functions, you will doubtless become aware that they are not completely independent of one another, nor are they necessarily done in any set sequence. Though they are primarily different types of activity, they are interdependent and interrelated. In an event that is classified as being primarily related to one function, elements of one or more of the others may be present. For example, in a worship service, proclamation may be a strong element; nurture and education may be involved; and elements of ministry may be present.

Pervading these functional areas in varying degrees are emphases such as family ministry, stewardship, missions development, and evangelism. They find expression appropriately through each function. To omit or underemphasize them is to fall short of the biblical norm for that function.

For Bold Mission Thrust to become a greater reality, churches need to place greater emphasis on functioning as God's people when away from the church building. If the lost are to be reached for Christ, more of a church's proclamation and witness and its ministry actions will have to occur when church members are dispersed out into the society, at work, in school, in the home, in the neighborhood, and in recreational and community activities.

The Tasks of a Church

Though functions are more specific statements of intentions than the mission statement is, they still are not sufficiently specific to be used for stating the work to be assigned to specific church programs. The more specific statements of intention are called tasks. Church tasks define the continuing activity performed by a church to carry out its functions in accomplishing its mission. They are detailed enough to be structured into programs of work for assignment to responsible leaders.

Church task statements are useful because they:

1. Reflect the ways in which a church will pursue its mission.

2. Provide an orderly division of a church's work.

3. Provide a clear definition of the continuing work of a church.

4. Provide a basis for structuring continuing programs and developing dated intentions of a church.

All church tasks should be consistent with a church's nature and mission. Taken together, they should be comprehensive of the total continuing work of a church. Each task should be limited to one specific kind of church activity.

Church tasks are performed by three types of church programs: basic programs, emphasis programs, and service programs.

Basic Program Tasks

A basic program encompasses the work in a cluster of tasks that are basic, continuing, and of primary importance to the total work of a church. It has significant organization and seeks to involve the total church in its work in regularly scheduled, ongoing activity, as well as in short-term projects. It maintains a membership roll. It coordinates its plans with those of emphasis and service programs through the churchwide planning/coordinating group (Church Council).

Based on this definition, what programs in your church would you classify as basic programs?

A   Out of years of study and experience, leaders of Southern Baptist Convention agencies have identified six basic programs in Southern Baptist churches. Here is a list of these programs and the tasks for which each is responsible.

Pastoral Ministries

1. Lead the church in the accomplishment of its mission.

2. Proclaim the gospel to believers and unbelievers.

3. Care for the church's members and other persons in the community.

4. Interpret and undergird the work of the church and the denomination.

Bible Teaching

1. Reach persons for Bible study.

2. Teach the Bible.

3. Witness to persons about Christ and lead persons into church membership.

4. Minister to persons in need.

5. Lead members to worship.

6. Interpret and undergird the work of the church and the denomination.

Church Training

1. Reach persons for discipleship training.

2. Orient new church members for responsible church membership.

3. Equip church members for discipleship and personal ministry.

4. Teach Christian theology and Baptist doctrine, Christian ethics, Christian history, and church polity and organization.

5. Train church leaders for ministry.

6. Interpret and undergird the work of the church and the denomination.

Music Ministry

1. Provide musical experiences in congregational services.

2. Provide church music education.

3. Lead the church to witness and minister through music.

4. Assist church programs in providing training in music skills and in consultation about music equipment.

5. Interpret and undergird the work of the church and the denomination.

Brotherhood

1. Engage in missions activities.

2. Teach missions.

3. Pray for and give to missions.

4. Develop personal ministry.

5. Interpret and undergird the work of the church and the denomination.

Woman's Missionary Union

1. Teach missions.

2. Engage in mission action and personal witnessing.

3. Support missions.

4. Interpret and undergird the work of the church and the denomination.

Emphasis Program Tasks

An emphasis program encompasses a task or cluster of tasks that deal with one or more continuing concerns of major importance in achieving a church's mission but which need to permeate all church programs as appropriate for their tasks. Because of its nature and importance, an emphasis program depends heavily on other programs, especially basic programs, to provide education and information about emphasis concerns through their ongoing program groups, regular meetings (including congregational services), and other channels of communication. You will notice that all the basic programs have a common task which makes them responsible for communicating information about the concerns of other programs.

An emphasis program has church-elected leaders as appropriate. It generally does not maintain an ongoing enrollment as base programs do. However, the church may choose to approve emphasis project groups or continuing special interest groups relating to emphasis concerns. Emphasis program plans involving other programs are coordinated with the plans of other programs through the

churchwide planning/coordinating group (Church Council).
Here is a listing of emphasis programs and their tasks.

1. Family Ministry
Minister to the distinctive needs of couples, parents and their children, senior adults, and single adults.

2. Stewardship
1. Develop Christian stewards.
2. Involve the church in supporting Cooperative Program ministries.

3. Evangelism
1. Engage the church in evangelism by developing a comprehensive church strategy of evangelism.
2. Involve church members in personal evangelism.
3. Reach persons for Christ through special events and mass evangelism.

4. Missions Development
1. Identify missions needs/opportunities.
2. Develop missions strategies to respond to unmet missions needs.
3. Estabish new churches.
4. Support establishment and strengthening of WMU and Brotherhood.

5. Vocational Guidance
Educate in Christian vocation and guide persons in church occupation choice and adjustment.

6. Student Ministry
1. Witness to persons about Christ.
2. Lead students into responsible church membershp.
3. Devleop ministries to persons.
4. Guide students in making life decisions.
5. Involve students in study of the Bible and Christian faith.
6. Involve students in missions.
7. Lead students to worship.
8. Build Christian fellowship.
9. Involve students in world issues and social action.

C. **Service Program Tasks**

A service program encompasses the work in a task or cluster of tasks that are supportive to the congregation and to other programs. A service program has organization but does not maintain an ongoing enrollment in regularly meeting groups for all or large subgroups of church members. Service program plans involving other programs are coordinated through the churchwide planning/coordinating group (Church Council). Here is a list of service programs and their tasks.

1. *Media Library*
1. Provide media and media library services.
2. Promote the use of media and media library services.
3. Train persons in media skills.

2. *Recreation Services*
Provide recreation methods, materials, services, and experiences that will enrich the lives of persons and support the total mission of the church.

3. *Administrative Services*
Assist the church to plan its program, manage its resources. and govern its life and work.

These programs are not the only ways Southern Baptists structure their work, but they have proved to be effective in many churches. These programs and tasks are used as a basis for designing the assistance that Southern Baptist Convention agencies make available to the churches.

✎ ::

Pause and Do: *Personal Learning Activity 3*
1. Write a mission statement for your church. (If the church has adopted a mission statement, use it.)
2. List the functions of the church. To which of the functions does your church need to give more attention in relation to Bold Mission Thrust?
3. List the programs of each type—basic, emphasis, and service—that exist in your church. What programs need to be strengthened (or organized) in relation to Bold Mission Thrust?

::: ✏

CHAPTER 4

Leading the Church Through Pastoral Ministries

When you see the expression *pastoral ministries,* do you first think of the work of your pastor? That is a good place to begin, for the pastor is the key leader in the pastoral ministries program. However, the work of pastoral ministries is not limited to what the pastor himself does.

There is an important difference in the words *pastoral* and *pastor.* *Pastor* denotes the role of one church leader. It is a functional role. Pastors are gifted and called by God's Spirit according to Ephesians 4:11. Not all ministry leaders are pastors, but all have a pastoral or shepherding role.[1]

As we have seen in reviewing New Testament passages about God's people in the church, all church members are ministers (see

Eph. 4:11-16). This is the New Testament ideal (see 1 Pet. 2:4-5, 9-10). Those called to special leadership ministry in the church are shepherd/pastoral ministers.

Use of the word *clergy* to apply to pastors and other staff ministers to distinguish them from laity is based more on church history than on New Testament teachings. The New Testament Greek word *laos* from which we get our word *laity* means "the people of God" or "God's people." It is an inclusive term that refers to all people who believe in and are committed to Jesus as Savior and Lord. This means that "laity" *(laos)* in the New Testament includes all church leaders such as pastors, other staff ministers, and deacons. From the New Testament use of *laos*, we understand that God's people are to be equipped and trained for ministry.[2] The pastor and other pastoral ministries leaders are responsible for equipping God's people for their mission.

Leadership—a Necessity

Joe Stacker, director of the Church Administration Department, Baptist Sunday School Board, has said: "Leadership is a must for a church. Without leadership nothing happens. An auto is inoperative without a trained driver. A computer can't compute without a programmer and an operator. A squad of soldiers might shoot one another without a sergeant. And a church is lacking without pastoral ministry leaders—leaders who know their role, task, and possible results."[3] A church that is to be on bold mission needs positive, effective leadership from the pastor and other pastoral ministries leaders.

Leaders in Pastoral Ministries

The earliest churches set aside respected and gifted persons to minister to them and lead them. The two stated officers were pastor (or overseer, elder) and deacons (see Phil. 1:1).

The pastor is the primary servant in a Southern Baptist church. He is the leader of the entire church in the accomplishment of its mission. He is also leader of the pastoral ministries team.

Deacons serve with the pastor as pastoral ministries leaders. They are ministers and must be able to perform such ministries as the church may require.

Many churches need additional vocational ministers such as ministers of music, associate pastors, ministers of education, ministers to age groups such as youth, ministers of recreation, and church business administrators. This is not out of harmony with the pattern of multiple leadership found in some New Testament churches. All of these are pastoral ministries leaders.

In addition to the ministry provided by pastors, staff ministers, and deacons, the Church Council is an important organizational element in the overall work of pastoral ministries. It serves as an administrative channel by which church pastoral ministers can provide leadership of the church's program. Church Council members serve in pastoral ministries whenever they are involved in planning and coordinating the work assigned by the church to the program each of them leads.

Some Southern Baptist churches are served by pastors and other staff leaders who are part-time or bivocational, meaning that they provide much of their own support by working at another occupation, as Paul did. As Bold Mission Thrust succeeds, thousands of new churches will be established, causing a significant increase in the number that can support only this kind of pastoral ministries leaders. This could lead to a strengthening of the biblical concept that all of God's people are ministers, but it will not lessen the need for God's people to have effective leaders in the church.

At times when a church is without a pastor or other vocational minister, responsibilities of that position may be carried by other church members. Christian ministry is not reserved for "professional clergy." There is to be a sharing of the ministry of the church among all believers whatever their roles or gifts. It is the gifting and calling of God which determines the particular service that individuals and groups perform. A commitment to the concept and practice of shared ministry will result in a closer working relationship for pastors, deacons, staff ministers, and other church members. It is not that one has his way over the other but that all allow Christ to have His way as Lord.[4]

The Tasks of Pastoral Ministries

The program of pastoral ministries is responsible for four church tasks that are basic activities of primary importance in moving a church toward the accomplishment of its mission. They require prophetic, priestly, consultative, and administrative activities by pastoral ministries leaders.

Pastoral ministries is an enabling and equipping program. As such, its fullest potential is realized as other church programs are effective and as the church is successful in carrying out its mission.

Task 1: Lead the Church in the Accomplishment of Its Mission
This task gives the pastor and other pastoral ministries leaders responsibility for helping all God's people in a church work together in ways that contribute to fulfilling the church's mission. It places great responsibility on them for the results a church achieves in fulfilling its mission. Successful group action requires leadership and responsive participation. This task does not mean that pastoral ministries leaders are to do all the work of church leaders, but it does provide an opportunity for the leaders to share the ministry. Through planning, preparing, praying, and proceeding, people are being saved, are growing, and are serving in a shared ministry. This expands the work of the church by pushing ministry out to every member.[5]

Leadership is accomplished through helping the church develop and maintain effective organization, through relating persons to persons and persons to tasks in a way that produces individual and church growth, and through building a personal and interpersonal climate in which persons desire to participate.

In giving leadership, pastoral ministries leaders will need to accomplish four essential actions on a continuing basis.

Motivate church members to experience a desire for growth.—
Pastoral ministries leaders can provide congregational services which present clearly the Bible's message of personal value, responsibility, and potential. Through their counseling, they can help persons discover personal value and develop a desire for growth. Through their personal contacts and in writing, they can share in-

formation that reveals the growth potential of the church. But to undergird and strengthen all other efforts, they need to show by example what it means to be a growing Christian.

2 *Guide the church in planning, coordinating, conducting, and evaluating its program activities.*—The pastor and other pastoral ministries leaders can preach and teach concerning the nature and functions of the church. By giving effective leadership in administration, they can help the church discover its priorities for ministry and express its specific desired outcomes in measurable goals and action plans. They can lead the church to develop effective organizational patterns, policies, and procedures tailored to meet the church's unique needs. They can develop an effective Church Council through which to coordinate the church's work.

Another important area of leadership is leading God's people to practice good Christian stewardship through which they provide adequate resources for the church's program activities and use them wisely.

Pastoral ministries leaders can also provide leadership by helping church officers, committees, and church programs accomplish their assignments effectively so that they will experience a sense of fulfillment and joy in their service.

3 *Maintain adequate communication with church members.*—The importance of adequate and accurate communication among God's people in a church can hardly be overemphasized. How often have you heard a church member say (or have you said), "Who made the decision to. . . ?" "That change relates to my work, but I wasn't consulted about it." "I wish they would check with me before scheduling conflicting activities." Or, "I don't feel that I know what is going on in my church." Such comments often reflect poor communication, and they certainly reflect feelings that do not contribute to strong fellowship and effective service in a church.

The pastor, deacons, other staff members, and church leaders who serve on the Church Council can set a pattern and an expectation of keeping church members well-informed about the church's life and work. They have opportunities to give and receive information in congregational services, through their personal counseling, when visiting in homes, and when participating in various church meetings and events. They can provide information through printed materials of various types, such as church bulletins, church papers or newsletters, letters, brochures, and posters.

Demonstrate personal commitment and appreciation.—In reviewing the needs of persons (chapter 2), we considered the human need to feel appreciated and valued. Pastoral ministries leaders can help meet this need of God's people by giving appropriate recognition in congregational services and by providing special recognition activities (dinners, receptions, fellowships, etc.) for groups of workers. Personal notes expressing appreciation and encouragement to program leaders and other individuals can heighten their enthusiasm and deepen their joy in service. Church Council meetings provide occasions for recognizing and expressing gratitude for good attitudes and significant efforts or accomplishments. Personal consultation and visits with families provide additional opportunities to express Christian love and appreciation. Wise leaders are generous in commendation which is deserved and active in forming constructive, encouraging relationships with persons whose performance does not merit praise. Helping persons to feel appreciated and valued will contribute to their growth in service and to stronger fellowship within the church.

"Pastoral ministries leadership must be positive, open, biblical, and shared. No one, from the pastor to the nursery coordinator, can assume he or she is in charge. Jesus is Lord of His church, and that's where all church leadership begins and ends."[6]

Task 2: Proclaim the Gospel to Believers and Unbelievers

This task places pastoral ministries leaders at the heart of a church's mission. *Proclaim* means "to announce in public, in private conversation, and through written communication." *Gospel* means "the good news of the person and work of Jesus Christ, as set forth in the Bible and experienced in the life of believers." It includes both the *kerygma,* the gospel which saves, and the *didache,* the teaching which edifies. The gospel is proclaimed in order that persons may know it, believe it, and experience its meaning in their lives.

Historically, churches have enlisted ministers who are committed, qualified, and gifted for proclaiming activities. But if the pattern of the early churches is to be followed, the proclamation of the apostles or ministers is to be augmented by the proclamation of others who serve with the ministers and by the proclamation of all believers who are to go everywhere spreading the word. Though pastor, deacons, other staff, and leaders of church programs have a heavy responsibility for proclaiming the gospel, it is a responsibility they share with all believers, all church members. In addition to being responsible for their own direct efforts, they are responsible for leading and equipping all church members to become proclaimers to the extent of their ability and opportunity.

In doing this task, pastoral ministries leaders need to accomplish five specific, essential actions.

1. *Discover needs for proclamation.*—To discover needs for proclamation, pastoral ministries leaders can use surveys which reveal the needs of church members and persons in the community. Interviews with leaders of other churches and denominations can provide fresh ideas. Consultation with leaders in church programs, personal and group counseling, and dialogue with groups or individuals can give pastor, deacons, and staff ministers helpful insights into the recognized needs for proclamation of the gospel.

2. *Discover and/or develop opportunities for proclamation.*—In exploring this task, let's try to avoid the serious mistake of equating proclamation with the preaching that goes on in regular services at the church. These services, of course, are prime times for proclaiming the gospel; and the preaching done there is a basic and indispensable part of a church's proclamation. But it is only a small part of the proclamation that pastoral ministries leaders and other church members must be involved in if Bold Mission Thrust is to become a reality in your church community and to the uttermost part of the earth.

To illustrate, if all the unbelievers who are in your regular services are won to the Lord in the near future, will there be a large increase in conversions and baptisms? Will there be many new converts who are not from church families?

Many, if not most, Southern Baptist churches are doing a better job of proclaiming the gospel to believers than to unbelievers. But does your church usually have more than half of the resident members present (not counting young children who are not yet church members) to hear the Word proclaimed in the Sunday morning worship service? If the answers to these questions are cause for deep concern, do we dare to face them and ask the Lord to help us do something bold about changing the answers?

Other opportunities for proclamation include special services such as revivals; Christian Home Emphasis; services of music and drama around special days such as Christmas, Easter, and Thanksgiving; and special projects such as January Bible Study and Baptist Doctrine Study.

Numerous churches are making good use of radio and television for proclaiming the gospel. These media have great potential for proclaiming the gospel to a generation who spends a significant amount of time listening to radio and viewing television. Some churches broadcast their regular worship service. Others produce programs designed to reach persons who might tune out a regular service. Others use programs prepared by the Radio and Television Commission or other agencies and sponsored by the church or in cooperation with other churches or the association. The availability of the Southern Baptist ACTS network gives churches and associations new opportunities to use television to reach out beyond the church building with effective proclamation.

Other approaches for proclaiming the gospel include articles and announcements in newspapers (more than announcing congregational services); making available various printed materials such as tracts, bulletins, leaflets, flyers, door hangers, Scripture portions, and brochures for use in proclamation by members; special evangelistic meetings sponsored in cooperation with other churches; special programs in shopping centers and resort areas; and inquirers' classes for unbelievers and for believers interested in church membership. Approaches for evangelistic proclamation would be planned as part of the church's comprehensive evangelism strategy discussed in chapter 9.

3. *Enlist audiences for proclamation.*—Churches should use a variety of methods for enlisting persons to hear the gospel proclaimed. Personal contacts and invitations continue to be among the most effective methods. Public announcements through print and elec-

tronic media and oral announcements where groups assemble for other purposes can have an impact. Taking the proclamation to where the intended hearers are, as in shopping centers, resorts, nursing homes, prisons, etc. should be given serious consideration.

4 *Conduct worship and congregational meetings in which the gospel is interpreted.*—In conducting congregational meetings in which the gospel is proclaimed, pastoral ministries leaders will do well to use a variety of approaches in addition to the traditional sermon and oral interpretation of the Bible. Vocal and instrumental music, personal testimonies, drama, dialogue, monologues, films, slides, video segments, and other innovative methods can be blessed by the Holy Spirit to communicate and bring response to the gospel.

5 *Evaluate proclamation.*—Pastoral ministers should evaluate proclamation efforts regularly. This can be done through meetings of the staff, deacons, Church Council, and worship planning committee and through conversation and dialogue with the people.

To be on Bold Mission God's people must not shrink from being bold in proclaiming the word by all worthy means. Timid clinging to traditional approaches of a past era will not equip God's people to be on Bold Mission. The gospel is changeless; the commission to share it is changeless; but the means by which God's people proclaim it must be the most up-to-date and effective that God makes available to us.

Task 3: Care for the Church's Members and Other Persons in the Community

Pastoral ministries leaders are responsible for helping the church develop an awareness of itself as a caring community and live out that awareness in response to persons' needs. They seek the involvement of all church members in individual and group expressions of love and concern. Pastoral ministries leaders are also responsible for providing shepherding and counseling services to persons in the church and community who have special needs. They lead the church in organizing its resources and making them available for meeting human needs but do not assume any responsibilities that can be cared for by other church members through church programs.

Care is feeling and demonstrating the expressed concern God has for all persons. It is the personal expression of God's love for all persons and for the whole person. Christians are persons in whom the love of Christ lives. A church should be known as a community of believers that expresses the love of Christ in relation to human need.

According to Joe Stacker: "Care for church and community is vital to all we do. Broken, hurting people are not difficult to find. They live in our homes and communities. The church seeks ways to establish mission action projects that reach out to those who hurt. Caring involves pastoral counseling, deacon family ministry, support from Sunday School classes, and individual support."[7]

In performing this task, pastoral ministries leaders need to accomplish these specific actions.

Discover the needs for care which should involve pastoral ministries leaders.—Pastoral ministries leaders can discover needs through visiting with individuals and families in their homes, through personal counseling, and through personal contacts in the course of daily life. They may provide opportunities for sharing information about personal needs in congregational services such as the midweek service or small-group meetings.

Conducting church and community surveys or interpreting available survey reports can supply much information about needs. Community agencies may have valuable information about community needs, and participants in church programs are another source of useful information.

Communicate concern and the availability of caring skills to persons in the church and community.—Pastoral ministries leaders can accomplish this action through preaching, visits to individuals and families in the church and community, and other personal contacts. Also, they may find it effective to initiate contacts with community agencies and persons in helping professions in the community.

Engage in caring activities.—Pastoral preaching and personal counseling are two major caring activities for pastoral ministries leaders. Also, they can:

• Administer church financial and other material resources to meet needs according to church policies and procedures.

• Make referrals to appropriate persons and agencies in the community and to church program organizations.

• Enlist the assistance of church members whose expertise is needed.

• Organize therapy groups with qualified leaders.

• Take action to change conditions in the community that contribute to personal and family crises.

• Provide an effective deacon ministry to persons and families.

• Direct personal reading programs that will help persons find solutions to personal problems.

4 *Provide for restorative and remedial discipline of church members.*—Caring actions like those already discussed which focus on concern for persons make it less likely that restorative or remedial discipline will be needed. But even when such actions are taken, problems may develop in church fellowship that need restorative discipline such as Paul described in Galatians 6:1.

Pastoral ministries leaders may initiate counseling with an individual whose conduct threatens the fellowship. If necessary, they may lead the church to consider action like that described by Jesus in Matthew 18:15-17 and by Paul in 1 Corinthians 5 regarding membership of an individual who cannot be reconciled to fellowship and whose conduct threatens the fellowship. If an unreconcilable member is separated from the membership, it should be in an effort to help him or her find fellowship with God that will be expressed in fellowship with people.

5 *Train persons for effective caring actions.*

6 *Evaluate caring activities.*—Pastoral ministries leaders can evaluate the results of caring actions through meetings of the staff, deacons, and Church Council; dialogue in congregational services; written surveys of the members; and dialogue with other caring professionals and organizations in the community.

A church that shows it cares for persons, and especially for those outside its membership, will have more opportunities for reaching the lost and unchurched as a result of its caring actions. The care a church expresses for its own members will deepen and strengthen the fellowship and will be a strong asset in drawing others into the fellowship of caring.

Task 4: Interpret and Undergird the Work of the Church and the Denomination

Though the pastoral ministries program shares this task with all other basic programs, its leaders have a heavy responsibility for implementing it because of the scope of the other pastoral ministries tasks and their role as key leaders.

Part of the success of pastoral ministries depends on interpreting and undergirding the work of the entire church and the denomination. If anyone in a church should know what is going on, a pastoral ministries leader should. They are responsible for sharing information about the work of their church and denomination so that persons can understand sufficiently, relate appropriately, and participate meaningfully. Church members and their families need to know about the work of the church locally and about its work through cooperation with other churches in the association, state convention, and the Southern Baptist Convention.

Congregational services provide an excellent setting for supporting the work of the church and the denomination. Sermons and worship bulletins can communicate important, informational, and inspirational messages or compelling features. For example, a project of Woman's Missionary Union, Brotherhood, or the Missions Development Council can be reported on effectively in both an informational and inspirational way. Special prayer activities and congregational service features undergird emphases like Bold Mission Thrust and specific projects within it such as Planned Growth in Giving.

Church newsletters and other printed materials can carry attractive, timely information about church and denominational life. Audiovisuals are also effective in presenting information.

Church Council meetings are useful for channeling information about church and denominational activities through all church programs as appropriate for their tasks. The Council can develop a coordinated communication plan for the entire church.

Through deacon ministry, deacons have many opportunities as they talk with church members to present information about the church and denomination, to correct misunderstandings, and to build goodwill and informed support for church and denominational activities.

Southern Baptists must work together toward worthy goals. Coordination and cooperation are possible only when the lines of communication are kept open between church members and denominational leaders.

✎ ::

Pause and Do: *Personal Learning Activity 4*

1. Who are the leaders in the pastoral ministries program?

2. Who is included in the term the *laos* of God?

3. List the church tasks of pastoral ministries.

4. List four ways your church might proclaim the gospel to unbelievers who don't usually attend your worship services.

::: ✉

---

[1]This introductory section draws from resource material prepared by Joe Stacker, director of Church Administration Department, Sunday School Board, for use in this book.

[2]Findley B. Edge, *The Doctrine of the Laity* (Nashville: Convention Press, 1985), p. 9.

[3]Stacker.

[4]Joe R. Stacker, "Doing Ministry Biblically: What the Bible Says" in Joe R. Stacker and Bruce Grubbs, *Shared Ministry: a Journey Toward Togetherness in Ministry* (Nashville: Convention Press, 1985), p. 16.

[5]Stacker, resource material.

[6]Ibid.

[7]Ibid.

CHAPTER 5

Sharing Christ Through Bible Teaching and Outreach

A church on bold mission needs to:
- Reach persons for Bible study.
- Teach the Bible.
- Witness to persons about Christ and lead persons into church membership.
- Minister to persons in need.
- Lead members to worship.
- Interpret and undergird the work of the church and the denomination.

If God's people in your church were offered a tried and tested way to accomplish these intentions, wouldn't you use it to maximum potential? The Bible teaching program is that "tried and tested way" to do all these things. It is simply God's people in a church organizing themselves to accomplish these biblical, basic, and specific intentions (tasks) that are vital to their God-given mission.

The Bible Teaching Program

Comparison of Bible teaching program tasks with the mission and functions of a church will lead you to see that through these tasks your church can place responsibility among its members for accomplishing basic work in all four church functions. The Bible teaching program provides the focus and the organization for evangelistic outreach to unsaved and unchurched persons. It calls your church members, their families, and all other persons within your church's reach to study the Bible—our written source of the gospel message, our guide for Christian growth and service, and our authority for faith and practice. It leads God's people to worship as individuals, as families, in small groups, and in the assembled congregation. It challenges them to minister to the needs of persons in the name of Christ and provides organization to help ministry happen. Its departments and classes provide a structure through which loving care, practical ministry, and Christian fellowship can find enabling support and expression. By serving as a channel of communication, it helps your church members to be informed participants in the life and work of your church locally and in its cooperative efforts with God's people in other churches of the association, state convention, and Southern Baptist Convention.

The Bible teaching program is more than Sunday School, but Sunday School is its primary organizational expression. For that reason, Sunday School is commonly used as a name for the Bible teaching program in Southern Baptist churches. However, as God's people look for bold and innovative ways to reach persons with the gospel, thinking in terms of the broader Bible teaching program concept will help them to reach beyond the limits of the Bible teaching that is done on Sunday morning at the church building. A church on bold mission will need to consider doing Bible teaching at other times and in other places.

Now, let's explore in greater depth the potential that each Bible teaching program task has for helping God's people be on bold mission with Him.

Tasks of the Bible Teaching Program

Task 1: Reach Persons for Bible Study

"Multitudes of ones" is a favorite expression of Harry Piland of the Baptist Sunday School Board, leader of Southern Baptists' Sunday School work, when he writes and speaks about those who need to be reached for Bible study and salvation. This expression helps us bring a general idea of a large number down to one person who needs the message of the Bible to become reality in daily experience. It refers to each person whom you and I must reach. The purpose of this task is to involve as many persons as possible in Bible study. Persons cannot be taught the Bible until they are involved in Bible study. The Sunday School reaches persons in order to share with them the good news of the gospel from the Word of God and the guidance and strength for daily living that the Word provides. We reach persons for Bible study because we believe the Holy Spirit will use God's Word to draw persons to Christ for salvation and lead them to grow in their commitment to live the gospel.

"There are millions who will die in their sin unless someone tells them about Jesus Christ. There are millions who will never study the Bible unless someone reaches out and involves them in Bible study. There are millions who will wander and drift aimlessly until finally they lose all hope and must face the judgment of God without Christ in their hearts."[1]

How many persons among the lost and unchurched millions are within reach of your church?

Who are the persons to be reached?—They may be thought of in several groups: unsaved persons, unchurched Christians, church members who are not in Bible study, and children of all these. But reaching people in these groups is not to be limited to those who are "just like us." People of different races, backgrounds, cultures, and languages also need God's message; and their number is growing rapidly throughout the United States. Those who do not have sight or hearing, who are mentally retarded, or who have other handicaps need God's Word. In short, the focus of Sunday School outreach must be all persons everywhere. Sunday School outreach should reach as far as God's love in Christ—to all persons.

In its reaching efforts, a church should not forget those who are enrolled but are frequently or chronically absent. Teachers, class officers, and class members should be alert and active in maintaining contact with these members and should work faithfully to reclaim them for the blessings of Bible study and Christian fellowship. Frequent communication with absentees may reveal opportunities to minister to spiritual or other needs that have developed in the member's life or family.

How are persons to be reached?—The primary approaches are visiting to enroll or cultivate, ministering to needs, and providing as many settings as possible in which to teach the Bible. Sunday School workers and members need to go to homes, businesses, tourist attractions, and any other places where they can find persons in need of Bible study. They should be encouraged to take advantage of day-to-day contacts and relationships to reach persons for Bible study.

It is the Sunday School's responsibility to locate prospects and keep an up-to-date file on each person who needs an invitation to Bible study or an evangelistic witness. Successful outreach and witness depend on the accuracy and availability of this information.

The Sunday School provides a ready-made organization through which to administer an ongoing program of visitation. Every department and class should have an effective outreach organization which regularly assigns responsibility for enlistment of prospects from an up-to-date prospect file. Thorough follow-up should ensure that assignments are completed, information is returned to the church, and significant information is carefully recorded in the prospect records for future use by other outreach workers.

Other effective ways to reach persons for Bible study are Outreach Bible Study, Bible Study Fellowships, starting new Sunday Schools, Vacation Bible Schools, mission Vacation Bible Schools, Backyard Bible Clubs, and special outreach efforts targeted to groups such as college students or ethnics. Scripture distribution is an effective way to locate prospects, cultivate them, and enlist them. The entrance of God's Word gives light. It motivates; it convicts; it stimulates action.

Beginning Outreach Bible Study—a new approach.—Outreach Bible Study groups are an effective means for reaching persons who are not enrolled in Bible study anywhere. Many of these persons are unsaved and not interested in attending Bible study or worship in a church setting. They can be invited to Bible study in a home, apartment, or office, with a capable leader who has been selected and trained by the church. WMU, Brotherhood, and the evangelism program will work with Sunday School in this effort. Bible study material prepared especially for these groups is available from the Baptist Sunday School Board. God's people who want to be on bold mission should strongly consider organizing as many Outreach Bible Study groups as the church can support with leadership and other resources.

Starting new Sunday Schools.—Southern Baptists are starting new Sunday Schools at a significant pace—8,760 between October 1, 1977 and September 30, 1985—but thousands more are needed. As a part of Bold Mission Thrust, Southern Baptists have set a goal of starting eight thousand new Sunday Schools between October 1, 1985 and September 30, 1990. Many of these new Sunday Schools will grow into churches, thus helping reach the goal of starting five thousand churches during the same period.

In addition to these ways of reaching persons, a church on bold mission should consider using public news media. Creative awareness articles in newspapers and spot announcements on television and radio can inform the general public of a church's concern for the community. Churches that have access to Southern Baptists' ACTS network can use it effectively to reach persons.

In today's society, especially in urban areas, some persons are difficult to reach because of hindrances such as restricted access to apartment buildings, homes not open to strangers, and college dormitory rules that limit personal contact with students. But God's Spirit is available and ready to help His people overcome such barriers if we exercise determination, patience, creativity, and most of all, faith.

Direct mail can be used in various ways to communicate with prospects. For example, church bulletins can be sent or cultivation materials mailed over a period of weeks. Such efforts can be reinforced by telephone calls. Any of these could open up the way for a visit as God leads.

Let me urge you to consider prayerfully whether some of these approaches should be given higher priority for reaching persons for Bible study in your church. We can be sure that God expects us to bring persons under the influence of His Word and that His power is available to help us do it. Our part as God's people is to be available and committed to the effort.

✎ ::

Pause and Do: *Personal Learning Activity 5*
   1. What plans does your church have to reach more persons for Bible study?
   2. Describe at least two approaches your church could use to reach more persons for Bible study. Share your ideas with the Sunday School director or outreach director.

::✏

Task 2: Teach the Bible

Though simply stated, this task has profound, life-changing meaning. It means that a church will involve persons in the study of God's written revelation, the Bible, and in the application of its meaning to all of life's activities and relationships.

The Bible is the textbook.—In *Basic Sunday School Work* Harry Piland wrote: "The Bible is the textbook of the Sunday School. While other lessons helps are used in preparation, it is the Bible that is studied; the written revelation of God is the Sunday School curriculum. We have a clear-cut and positive call to teach the Bible to the members and prospects of the Sunday School. Young and old, rich and poor, educated and uneducated—everyone can profit from a diligent, regular study of the Bible. Every person needs to study the Bible."[2] The Sunday School Department of the Baptist Sunday School Board provides many support materials to assist the church and its teachers in choosing their approaches to Bible study and developing their curriculum plan. But they are all intended to help the teacher teach the Book, the Bible.

Bible content is applied to life.—Teaching Bible content is essential and should never be neglected or taken lightly. But teaching the Bible goes beyond learning facts and information to understanding the message of God and how it is to be applied in life. The teaching/ learning experience must help learners discover for themselves how Bible truths apply to their activities and relationships. Bible teaching must include a strong emphasis on laying foundations for Chrisitan conversion and leading persons to faith in Christ.

Why do we teach the Bible?—Our Lord instructed His people to make disciples and teach them to observe His commandments. Through teaching the Bible we are obedient in doing both. We teach that persons, under the leadership of the Holy Spirit, may be led to respond to God with maturing faith, love, and obedience. We do not educate an individual into a positive response to God, but Bible study is an invaluable aid in leading a person to accept God's love. As Harry Piland wrote in *'Til Millions Know:*

> In addition to the need for knowing Christ as personal Savior, people need a continuing vital relationship with Christ, a Christian understanding of life, and a growing Christian experience. These can be provided by a good Bible teaching program in a church. Such teaching is indeed vital to the life of the church. A church must be gripped by the gospel if it is to be an effective force for Christ in the world. Otherwise, its members forget who they are, how they are to live, and what they are commissioned to do.
>
> [The Bible] helps us understand the lordship of Christ over the church. The Bible is central to understanding the mission of the church.
>
> The Bible gives the pattern for human conduct. It speaks to all the basic issues of life. It is for all ages and all people. It is truly a book for the whole world and for each person in the whole world. It is a book of hope and comfort, courage and strength. When applied, the message of the Bible will mold Christian character and produce families of enduring quality.[3]

Who is to be taught the Bible?—All church members, their families, and all others in the community except those who are involved in the Bible teaching programs of other churchs are potential students. How effective has your church been in involving these groups in Bible study?

Who is to teach?—Persons carefully and prayerfully selected, elected, and trained by the church can teach in the Bible teaching program. A teacher should feel that God has led him or her into the high calling of teaching. He or she should have a sense of deep commitment to the task and to regular preparation—physically, mentally, and spiritually. A teacher's life should be an example of what is taught and a model of integrity, character, honesty, and truthfulness. No matter how much other preparation is done, the seeds of failure are already sown if a teacher does not prepare spiritually through prayer and meditation to see the counsel, wisdom, guidance, and power of the Holy Spirit. The Holy Spirit teaches also.

High on the list of desirable qualities for a teacher is a loving, caring heart which is expressed beyond the classroom in acts of concern and ministry. It motivates the teacher to come to know each class member as a person with unique needs and learning styles. "People do not come to Christ by the carload or by the family; they come one at a time. Salvation and discipleship are individual and personal."[4]

When and where do we teach?—In most churches, the vast majority of Bible teaching occurs in Sunday School on Sunday morning in the church building. Both Christians and non-Christians are taught the Bible together in the same classes and departments in an ongoing plan of Bible study. This is basic in a church's Bible teaching program. But numerous other opportunities are also available for churches that want to be on bold mission in Bible teaching. Some examples of these are Vacation Bible School; mission Vacation Bible Schools; Backyard Bible Clubs; neighborhood Bible study groups; weekday Bible study groups at the church building or in homes, nursing homes, or apartment buildings; Outreach Bible Study groups; Bible study fellowships; Bible study projects such as January Bible Study and Bible conferences; radio and television studies; Bible study in camp, retreat, or resort settings; and special study groups for college students.

Task 3: Witness to Persons About Christ and Lead Persons into Church Membership

Is there any activity dearer to the heart of our Savior or more in the center of our mission as God's people than this task? Here is Harry Piland's answer to that question:

> However great our desire for people to come to know Jesus Christ as Savior, it is not as great as Christ's desire. Whatever the depth of our concern and love for people, it pales into insignificance compared to the love of Christ. The truth is, our concern springs from His love, our compassion from His example, our witness from His command. Southern Baptists have always been concerned about people. . . . It has been our sincere conviction that each person is important and savable. We truly want people to study the Bible. We want people to hear the gospel story. We want them to know who Jesus is, what He did, and why He did it. With all our hearts, we want them to respond in repentance and faith to Him.[5]

The purpose of this task is to involve Sunday School workers and members in discovering persons who are not Christians, cultivating them, witnessing to them personally and through teaching, and encouraging them to accept Christ as Savior. It also includes teaching and witnessing to lay foundations for Christian conversion. Because new Christians and church members not affiliated with a church need the fellowship of a body of believers, this task seeks to involve Sunday School workers and members in reaching such persons for church membership.

As important as reaching persons for Bible study is, the work of the Sunday School is incomplete until the teachers, officers, and other members follow through by sharing their faith. This should happen day by day throughout the year as believers say to those who don't know Christ as Savior: "I have experienced Jesus Christ in personal faith, and He is my Savior. He can be yours, too. Let me share this good news with you." Telling others about Christ is not the exclusive business of the ordained ministers or a few devoted people in a church. The Bible teaches that it is the responsibility of all of God's people.[6]

Pause and Do: *Personal Learning Activity 6*

1. Notice the simple approach to witnessing presented in the preceding paragraph. Do church members believe that witnessing is such a specialized skill that they must have special training before they are "qualified" to witness? Of course, training will improve their skills, but isn't the basic qualification a vibrant, personal, saving relationship with Christ—a daily experience of Christ that cries out to be shared? Do we need to begin here in motivating persons to witness? (No written answer required for individual study or makeup work.)

2. What could be done in your church to involve 10 percent more of your church members in personal witnessing within the next six months? (Written answer for individual study or makeup work.)

The essence of the work of the Sunday School is to provide a climate for continual personal witnessing in the class session on Sunday and throughout the week. Unreached persons must be made aware of the love and concern of persons who are seeking to witness to them. Visiting to cultivate friendship, ministering to the needs of persons, teaching the Bible evangelistically, and making faith-sharing visits are effective methods to be used to win unsaved persons to Christ and to lead unchurched persons to join a church.

Witnessing and winning involve going to homes, businesses, or any other places where there are persons who need the gospel. Witnessing also includes using every appropriate opportunity in the classroom to share the need for salvation and to encourage response to the gospel message.

Most pastors rely heavily on the Sunday School organization to cultivate evangelistic prospects, visit to witness, and promote attendance in revivals and other evangelistic meetings. This is an important way the Sunday School witnesses.

In addition to these methods, Sunday School members are encouraged to take advantage of day-to-day contacts and relationships to witness to persons about Christ and church membership. This type of witnessing will help transform Bold Mission Thrust from words on paper into life-changing experiences!

All Sunday School witnessing efforts should be planned as part of the church's comprehensive evangelism strategy discussed in chapter 9, "Reaching Persons for Christ."

Task 4: Minister to Persons in Need
This task means that officers, teachers, and other members of the Bible teaching program will be involved in helping one another and other persons in the church and community. *Minister* means "to meet the needs of persons and families in the Spirit of Christ." *Members in need* are those persons enrolled in the Bible teaching program and anyone within the scope of a ministering member's influence. The primary thrust of this task is on ministry to persons who are members of or prospects for the Bible teaching program, not on specialized target groups within the community. (Specialized target groups are a primary concern of the mission action and missions activities of Woman's Missionary Union, Brotherhood, and Missions Development in churches that have these programs.)

What does ministry include?—Ministry involves putting into practice the teachings of the Bible. Both crisis and continuing ministries are included. It includes a Christian life-style that is developed and practiced in small class or department groups. The ministry may take the form of personal service, concrete acts of caring expressed in material support, encouraging words, affirmation, prayer, or simply taking the time to listen. Such ministries can be especially meaningful in times of illness, grief, family problems, job loss, and serious material loss such as results from fire or other disasters. This task is at the heart of a loving, caring fellowship.

How is ministry encouraged and supported?—Follow-through activities in curriculum units in Sunday School, Vacation Bible School, or undated studies may motivate persons to minister. A functioning adult ministry organization in classes—activities leader, group leaders—can guide and support ministry efforts. Sunday School class projects such as class meetings, department socials, and fellowship periods can help build fellowship *(koinonia)* and create warmth and acceptance of one another. Activities by individual members and small groups of members may result from Bible learning experiences. Teaching approaches can foster openness, trust, sharing, and the developing of warm, human relationships.

The Sunday School organization can be involved in the annual Christian Home Emphasis and other Family Ministry activities. It can work with other church programs and with referral systems on campuses to discover and meet the needs of college students and involve them in ministering. The Cradle Roll ministry and the Homebound ministry provide many opportunities for ministry.

Through the Sunday School organization God's people can express Bible teachings in daily living by ministering in the name of Christ. In so doing, they will be faithful to both the example and the instructions of the Master. The loving acts of ministry will present numerous opportunities for sharing a witness with unbelievers and believers.

✎ ::

Pause and Do: *Personal Learning Activity 7*
   1. Describe two recent instances in which needed ministries have been performed through your Sunday School.
   2. Describe two needs among your church members or in your community that could be met through this Sunday School task.

::

Task 5: Lead Members to Worship

The Bible teaching program is responsible for leading its members to worship. Every class and department should be concerned about the participation of its members in public and private worship because worship is a vital part of the life of a growing Christian and a strong church.

This task includes providing motivation for persons to participate in personal, family, and church worship experiences. (The meaning of worship is discussed in chapters 1 and 3.) Its purpose is the spiritual renewal and growth toward maturity of individual members and the strengthening of Christian fellowship among group members and families.

Nothing can take the place of congregational worship. We are clearly taught the significance of worship in both Testaments. The Psalms are filled with references to the joy and blessings of worship.

Every Christian needs a daily period for individual worship in order to grow in insight, understanding, and Christian character. That is why the Sunday School encourages its members to feed on the Word, meditate, and pray daily.

The Sunday School also encourages family worship. As families read the Bible, discuss its meaning, and pray for strength, they experience growth in their relationship with Christ and with one another, gain deeper understanding, receive help in solving problems, and strengthen family ties.[7]

The Sunday School accomplishes this task by providing materials to assist individuals and families in worship, planning experiences to motivate persons to read the Bible daily and to worship, and promoting participation in opportunities to worship.

Pause and Do: *Personal Learning Activity 8*
   1. List specific ways your Sunday School emphasizes individual and family worship.
   2. Describe two things your Sunday School or church might do to encourage individual and family worship.

Task 6: Interpret and Undergird the Work of the Church and the Denomination

The Bible teaching program shares this task with the other five basic programs. But because its enrollment and attendance are usually larger than those of any other educational organization, it carries a major responsibility for the task. It has the organization through which the concerns of other programs can be communicated and supported.

For example, when the church is involved in a revival, a stewardship campaign, a family life emphasis, a Church Training event such as Baptist Doctrine Study, or weeks of prayer and special offerings for home and foreign missions, the Sunday School can make a major contribution by giving enthusiastic support and participation. It is a major means of interpreting a church's ministry budget and encouraging members to pledge their support for it. The Bible teaching program is not an organization apart from the church. It is the church organized to do specific tasks, and through this particular task it is committed to giving appropriate support to every concern of the church.

A Vision of the Sunday School on Bold Mission

To summarize our focus on Sunday School, let's consider these words of testimony and vision from Harry Piland:

> "I have been inspired and have grown in Christ because of the church and the Sunday School. For twenty-five years I served as a staff member in churches. I am and have been richly blessed; so, with gratitude, I say that I love the church and I love the Sunday School.
>
> Because of that love, I have a vision—a vision for the churches and Sunday Schools of the Southern Baptist Convention, a vision for each one of the . . . individual churches, and a vision for all of our church families and our Sunday School families. . . .
>
> I see churches and Sunday Schools gaining a new appreciation of commitment to Christ's mission. I see Sunday School workers and members sharing Christ with the countless multitudes in our nation. I see Christ being shared in offices, businesses, schools, neighborhoods, and families. I see Sunday Schools doing regular evangelistic visitation—multitudes of persons coming to Christ. I have a vision of our Sunday Schools coming to a unique and life-changing understanding of ministry. I see us caring for and loving the hungry, outcast, and lonely persons for whom our Lord had great compassion.
>
> What are your dreams for your church? Do you have a vision of what can happen in your church through its Sunday School? . . .
>
> Visions are seen with faith, the eyes of the soul. . . . God's Holy Spirit is the source and interpreter of our dreams for the future. Let the Holy Spirit give you a vision of what your Sunday School can do and then empower you and your co-workers to bring the dream to reality![8]

Then God's people at your church will truly be on bold mission with the Lord to do your part toward having ten million persons enrolled in Bible study in Southern Baptist Bible teaching programs by 1990 and twelve million by 1995. How many of those should be in your Sunday School and other Bible teaching units?

[1]John R. Bisagno and Harry M. Piland, 'Til Millions Know (Nashville: Convention Press, 1983), pp. 43-44.

[2]Harry M. Piland, Basic Sunday School Work (Nashville: Convention Press, 1980), p. 27.

[3]Bisagno and Piland, pp. 63-65.

[4]Ibid., p. 75.

[5]Larry Shotwell and Harry M. Piland, The Adult Challenge: Sunday School Outreach (Nashville: Convention Press, 1985), pp. 7-8.

[6]Adapted from Reginald M. McDonough, comp., A Church on Mission: an Intentional Response to the Needs of the Eighties (Nashville: Convention Press, 1980), pp. 89-90, 98-99.

[7]Adapted from Piland, p. 29.

[8]Ibid, pp. 30-32.

CHAPTER 6

Equipping God's People Through Discipleship Training

Equipping God's people for discipleship is essential to the success of Bold Mission Thrust. A full understanding of the biblical concept of discipleship will guide God's people in their efforts to be on bold mission.

What Does It Mean to Be a Disciple?

Writing in *Discipleship Training: a Church Training Manual.* Roy Edgemon, leader of our Southern Baptist Program of Church Training Development, begins the answer to this question by quoting the Great Commission, "Go therefore and make disciples of all the nations, baptizing them in the name of the Father and the Son and the Holy Spirit, teaching them to observe all that I commanded you;

and lo, I am with you always, even to the end of the age!" (Matt. 28:19-20, NASB).

Christians have called this passage the Great Commission. It is called great because it is God's blueprint for His plan for the ages. Jesus calls the church to make disciples as its members go thoughout the world.

Jesus chose the word *disciple* to refer to those who believed in Him and followed Him. The word *disciple* appears more than 250 times in the New Testament. *Disciple* comes from the Greek word *mathetes* which means a learner or a pupil. Thus, to believe in Christ and become His disciples is to make a lifelong commitment to learn from Him.

Disciples were those who had made a deliberate choice to follow Christ, to share in His ministry and life-style, and to proclaim the kingdom of God. Discipleship in the New Testament was serious. Becoming a disciple was exciting, challenging, and life changing.

A disciple's faith in Jesus becomes the stack pole around which all of life is organized. Jesus said this kind of commitment would bring abundant, overflowing life. However, He also stressed that the disciple's life would not always be easy.

The verb form of disciple that is used in this passage indicates a responsibility to enlist others as learners or disciples. The imperative of the passage is not in the word *"go"* but in the words *"make disciples."* The ultimate objective is made plain in the phrase *"all the nations."* After persons have believed and become disciples, the church is to baptize them and teach them everything that Jesus commanded.

Jesus taught that discipleship included a commitment to study and growth. He said, "If ye continue in my word, then are ye my disciples indeed" (John 8:31). Discipleship is a process of development based on the Word of God. Jesus expected His followers to learn His commands and to obey them in their lives.

Jesus also taught that a disciple allows God's love to permeate his relationships with other people. Jesus said, "By this shall all men know that ye are my disciples, if ye have love one to another" (John 13:35). The disciples' love for Jesus is viewed in the light of their love for others. John wrote, "Beloved, let us love one another: for love is of God; and every one that loveth is born of God, and knoweth God" (1 John 4:7).[1]

What Is Our Mandate from God?

Your church's training program takes its mandate from the New Testament. In Ephesians 4:11-16, Paul set forth major themes of Christian discipleship.

Paul called the church to equip all its members ("saints") by enabling them to grow toward Christian maturity measured by Christ Himself. Such equipping of the members will cause the church to be built up as a community of love because all of its members ("each individual part") are functioning as God intended. Personal and corporate spiritual vitality are interrelated. An individual cannot grow to full spiritual stature while separated from the fellowship of other believers within the church. At the same time, God's people as a body of believers cannot grow to full spiritual stature without growth and renewal in the life of individual believers.

We begin the Christian life as spiritual babes, but to remain spiritual infants is against the nature of faith and contrary to God's will for His people. Stunted growth in discipleship can cause various immature behaviors that damage the fellowship and influence of the church and thereby hinder God's people from being on bold mission with Him. Spiritual infants are as helpless in the spiritual storms of life as little children trying to control a boat in the midst of a storm (see Eph. 4:14).

A growing believer is never satisfied or complacent but constantly strives for the quality of life described by Paul as "the fruit of the Spirit is love, joy, peace, longsuffering, gentleness, goodness, faith, meekness, temperance" (Gal. 5:22-23). The whole body of the church is to be involved in this growth journey. The church is responsible for developing believers in spiritual maturity.

Paul wrote that each part of the body must work properly by doing its individual job (see Eph. 4:16). Gymnasts perform seemingly impossible feats of skill and strength with grace and beauty because every part of the body is disciplined to support the whole. When a church will pay the price to train and develop the body of Christ, then the working energy of each individual member combines to perform the work of the church.

What Is the Work of Church Training?

The Church Training program is concerned with equipping "all God's people for the work of Christian service, to build up the body of Christ" (see Eph. 4:12, GNB). It is designed to accomplish this through the six church tasks discussed in the remainder of this chapter.

Task 1: Reach Persons for Discipleship Training

The purpose of this task is to discover, enlist, and enroll as many persons as possible in discipleship training. A church must make deliberate-and well-planned efforts to involve persons in discipleship training. Reaching does not happen automatically just because an age group is provided for on Sunday evening or because an interesting study is offered.

Few church members take initiative to change their Sunday evening or other habit patterns to become involved in discipleship training without being invited, encouraged, and/or challenged by someone who is involved. The attitude sometimes voiced by church members that "they know we have Church Training at 5:45; if they're interested, they'll come!" will not grow a strong training program. It communicates to church members and their families that "we don't care enough about having you in discipleship training to put out any effort to call you to involvement." Is that attitude consistent with what it means to be God's people and to be on bold mission with Him?

The pastor and other leaders must take specific, effective actions to plan studies and activities that will develop believers in all aspects of discipleship as defined above.

To accomplish this task Church Training leaders need to carry out these essential actions on a continuing basis:

1. Discover persons in need of discipleship training.
2. Establish a caring relationship with them.
3. Enroll them in discipleship training.

4. Maintain continuing contact with those who are enrolled.

Visiting to cultivate or enroll, ministering to needs, and providing various settings and approaches to discipleship training are primary methods to be used by the Church Training program to involve persons in discipleship training. Persons may be reached through both planned and spontaneous actions.

Some of the more specific planned approaches that many churches find useful are:

• Growth plans and projects.

• Comparison of church membership and Church Training rolls to discover by name persons not enrolled in discipleship training.

• Assignment of responsibility for enlistment of prospects to Church Training groups and departments.

• Regular, ongoing communication of Church Training activities and studies to entire church membership.

• Visitation.

• Other approaches such as correspondence/mail; social activities; camps, retreats, conferences; tours; projects; and special approaches targeted to students or special interest groups.

Discipleship training activities will help Christians to grow in Christlikeness, in their ability to apply biblical truth to every area of life, in responsibilty for sharing the Christian faith, and in responsible church membership. Every Christian should be reached and involved in discipleship training because the entire body suffers when one believer fails to grow as a disciple. Increased attendance in training activities has several benefits to the church, but the primary purpose of Church Training is to carry out the Great Commission—to equip God's people to be on bold mission!

✎ ::

Pause and Do: *Personal Learning Activity 9*

1. List and describe briefly the special efforts your church has made within the last year to involve more persons in discipleship training.

2. (Answer only if the answer to number 1 is "None.") If there has not been any special effort to enlist members in training, what does that suggest to you?

::⊜

Task 2: Orient New Church Members for Responsible Church Membership

To start people on the road to discipleship, a church should orient new members in ways that will help them become responsible members. Both new converts and those who come on promise of letter or by statement need to understand and appreciate the opportunities and responsibilities of church membership.

This task includes helping the new church member understand the church as the body of Christ, the essential relationship of the member to the body, and the personal significance of every member. It also means assisting each new member in becoming fully incorporated into the body and in being introduced to the lifelong task of developing as a disciple. Recognition of the lordship of Christ and the member's servant role are likewise inherent in this task.

A church needs to make clear to every new member that he or she is expected to be a functioning member of the body of Christ, the church, and is covenanting with God's people to be a disciple involved in worship, proclamation, and witness; nurture and education; and ministry in the name of Christ. Our Lord does not intend for churches to have spectator or inactive members. But if a church does not provide any specific way to acquaint each new member with the opportunities and responsibilities of membership in that church at the time of joining, what basis does it have to call on the member later to live up to what membership means?

The growth of the new Christian depends on an understanding and appreciation of both the opportunities and responsibilities of church membership. The effectiveness of the church in the purpose of God depends on each member's being able to identify and develop his or her spiritual gifts.

Responsibility for this task is to be carried out by leaders selected and elected according to the church's plan. To ensure that this task is carried out effectively, Church Training leaders will need to take these essential actions:

1. Involve leaders and members of the church in the decision to conduct new church member orientation.

2. Analyze training needs periodically.

3. Provide leadership, organization, resources, facilities, and

time necessary to involve all new members in an appropriate training experience.

4. Enlist and train counselors.

5. Create a climate of expectation that all new members will participate.

6. Provide for transition from new church member orientation into follow-up training for Christian service.

Church Training leaders will need to provide counseling, training in Christian basics, and training in church membership leading to follow-up training for service and leadership. Both individual and group training can be utilized. It can be conducted on Sunday evenings and/or at such other times as the church may deem appropriate to meet the schedules of those who need to be involved. Much of this task will be accomplished in sessions at the church building; but some may be done in homes, retreat settings, and other places determined by the church.

Approaches churches have found useful in implementing this task include:

• Use of trained counselors at the point of decision.

• The use of encouragers or one-to-one leaders with new converts in cooperation with Sunday School, evangelism, and other church programs.

• Training materials designed for individual, one-to-one, and group study.

• Variations in materials, schedules, and training approaches essential to involve all new church members.

• Public recognition of those completing new church member training.

• Continuing emphasis on the concept of discipleship.

✎ ::

Pause and Do: *Personal Learning Activity 10*
1. Evaluate your church's process for receiving new members, orienting them, and helping them become functioning members.

2. What relationship do you see, if any, between the way a church receives, orients, and incorporates new members and the percentage of inactive members it has?

::⬄

**Task 3: Equip Church Members for Discipleship and Personal
Ministry**

Church members need to be equipped to function as Christians in
all aspects of life and thus fulfill their purpose as members of the
body of Christ. The primary focus of this task is on developing
understandings, skills, and relationships that all church members
need in order to be effective Christian disciples and to help build up
the church. Members need to learn how to practice the servant role
in leadership and ministry responsibilities.

Discipleship is the Christian's lifelong commitment to the person,
teaching, and spirit of Jesus Christ. Life under Jesus' lordship involves progressive learning, growth in Christlikeness, application of
biblical truth to every area of life, responsibility for sharing the
Christian faith, and developing spiritual gifts for personal ministry
and responsible church membership. *Personal ministry* is the Christian's response to human need as prompted by the spirit of Jesus
and *agape* love.

This task and the next one are usually implemented together
through a church member training organization. Leaders selected
and elected according to the church's plan are the persons assigned
responsibility for providing various types of training opportunities.
Learning experiences can be provided through group and individual studies and other activities in a continuing Church Training
organization, in short-term projects, in individual and one-to-one
study programs, and in retreat and conference settings.

Other possibilities for training approaches include a continuing
emphasis on Bible skills, guided reading programs, camps, retreats,
conferences, and projects; and cooperative training opportunities
with other churches, such as Baptist associational projects.

**Task 4: Teach Christian Theology and Baptist Doctrine,
Christian Ethics, Christian History, and Church Polity
and Organization**

Christians move toward maturity as they are taught. This task is
designed to involve learners in meaningful exploration of the real-
ities of the Christian faith and life in the subject areas named. The
learning experiences provided will help each person (1) to develop a

valid system of beliefs about God and His relationship to man (Christian theology), (2) to grow in Christian character and the ability to express and apply it in every relationship of daily living (Christian ethics), (3) to discover and appropriate meaning and values in Christian history; and (4) to explore church polity and organization and the ways Baptists work together in achieving Christ's objectives for churches.

As believers become better grounded in doctrine, they can spot the flaws in the claims of cults and sects. Their discipleship becomes richer and more effective. As they study ethics, they begin to apply biblical standards to decisions they must make in their daily lives. Their church's doctrine, traditions, business meetings, and particular emphases such as missions offerings become more understandable as they learn more of the history and heritage of Southern Baptists. They can make better informed choices about serving, giving, and otherwise participating in a Southern Baptist church as they learn the purpose of the various programs of Southern Baptists.

Much of this training is done on Sunday evening prior to the evening worship hour. This is a prime time in most churches and its importance should be kept before church leaders and members on a continuing basis. Some churches find it wise to schedule training on Sunday morning, before or after Bible teaching. Training may be done at times other than Sundays. Churches may find it necessary to schedule training for other days of the week in order to meet the training needs of church members. Some of these groups may meet at places other than the church building.

Periodic surveys of training needs among members will guide leaders in providing training opportunities to meet specific needs. Also, leaders should guide members in finding opportunities to apply knowledge, understanding, and skills they have gained through their training.

Task 5: Train Church Leaders for Ministry
Every pastor and leader knows that a strong church does not develop quickly. A church must have a continuing plan to train church leaders. Providing enough qualified workers in a church is a

perennial need. Providing training for leaders grows out of the biblical concept of volunteer leadership in a church. This concept is consistent with Christ's call to everyone for discipleship and ministry.

Through this task a church can provide general training for any type of leadership role commonly held by church members: potential leaders, new leaders, and experienced leaders. Training results in church members' developing increased competence to serve effectively and efficiently. As members are equipped to serve, some show leadership potential. Training enables potential leaders to gain an understanding of the type of leadership roles, both formal and informal, in which they are most likely to be effective. Specific training for a particular program's leaders is done by or in consultation with the leadership of that program as requested by them.

Potential leader training provides basic knowledge and understanding and develops basic skills in the general area of church leadership.—Potential leader training courses are offered primarily for older youth and adults who are not yet enlisted to serve in specific places of leadership.

New leader training enables a person to function in a specific leadership role and is conducted in cooperation with other church programs.—This training is needed by a leader to achieve a basic level of performance. It may be given when a person expresses an interest in a specific role, after election to a specific leadership position but before beginning to function in that position, or as soon as possible after beginning to function in a specific leadership position.

Experienced leader training enables a person who is already a leader to improve or gain additional knowledge, understanding, skills, or attitudes, or to develop as a leader beyond the point of functioning in a specific job.—Some experienced leader training cuts across program lines. For example, some training may be needed by all children's workers or all youth workers. Other training may be needed by all who have administrative responsibilities or who need to develop skills in group leadership. Another example is the course for training Sunday School workers in evangelistic skills.

Content for leader training includes introductory courses in church leadership, personal development of the leader's spiritual life, understanding work with age levels and special groups in a church, and developing general leadership skills. The Church Training program also provides training in the administration of church programs and training for church-elected or group-elected leaders of special projects and activities, as requested by leaders of other programs.

One or more persons should be selected and elected by the church to be responsible for discovering, recruiting, and training church leaders.

Task 6: Interpret and Undergird the Work of the Church and Denomination

Church Training shares this task with other basic programs. It uses its organization as a channel to help inform church members about all matters of interest to the church, whether it be the church's revival or attendance at a state Baptist convention. Performance of this task helps church members participate more meaningfully in the life and work of their church and denomination.

When information flows freely, people get along better with one another, become more involved in appropriate activities, give more generously, and more strongly support the various goals and activities of their church and cooperative efforts with other churches.

What Is Your Church Doing to Equip Members for Bold Mission?

As you think about that question, consider these words of Roy Edgemon, director of the Church Training Department, Sunday School Board:

> I dream of the day when Southern Baptist churches will spend quality time in equipping their people to live the Christian life. I dream of a day when the church will train its people to do the work of ministry. Paul gives us the high goals for discipleship in the local church in Ephesians 4:13-16.

Our training program for a church must be designed in such a way as to meet the needs of the new Christian and to equip lay members for specific ministries. It must be broad enough to range from a basic kindergarten of faith all the way to an intensive lay seminary.

We must train the best evangelism army that has ever taken the field of battle in all of Christian history. This evangelism must be intentional in that it trains people to go out and find the lost. It must be integrated in that the pew and the pulpit are of the same mind to seek and save the lost as the mandate of Christ. It must have integrity as those who come to Christ will be carefully and lovingly counseled in such a way as to establish them in their faith. It must be so designed in the local church that the new convert is nurtured to a point of involvement and commitment to the lordship of Christ. As Southern Baptists we have an organization that can do these things. We have the best resources that any people ever had in all the history of Christianity.

We must do this work. We must not let our discipleship ministry slip from our hands. We will do this work with renewed commitment because it is God's will that we help people to be saved and to grow up to the full stature of Christ.[2]

✎ ::

Pause and Do: *Personal Learning Activity 11*
Use the information in this chapter to evaluate your Church Training program.

1. Which of these six Church Training tasks are being accomplished most effectively by your church in equipping God's people for bold mission?

2. Which ones are weak or not being done at all?

3. What do you think your church should do to involve more members in discipleship training?

::

---

[1]Roy Edgemon, *Discipleship Training: a Church Training Manual* (Nashville: Convention Press, 1986). Parts of this chapter are adapted from chapter 1 and from material especially prepared for this book.

[2]Ibid.

CHAPTER 7

Involving God's People
Through the Music Ministry

"Let the word of Christ dwell in you richly in all wisdom; teaching and admonishing one another in psalms and hymns and spiritual songs, singing with grace in your hearts to the Lord" (Col. 3:16). That biblical instruction, coupled with the needs of people, reminds us of the importance of an effective Music Ministry to a church. The purpose of the Music Ministry is to glorify God, edify His children, and lead persons to a saving knowledge of Jesus Christ. Music, of all the arts, has long been imbedded in the heritage of Judeo-Christian worship. As a means of individual and corporate spiritual expression, music has been, is, and will continue to be a significant part of the life of God's people in the church.

What has church music contributed to your Christian life? to the life of your church? Are there certain hymns, gospel songs, or anthems that have a special meaning to you, that bring back vivid memories of deeply meaningful experiences in your Christian life? For example, was there an invitation hymn that helped move you to public decision, a prayer song that helped you commune with the Lord in a unique way, or a choir number that left you caught up in the praise and adoration of a loving God and ready to listen to his specific word for you?

Do you remember a solo that helped you understand and express your own spiritual longings or commitment; a hymn of comfort whose words and melody were used by the Spirit to minister gently and lovingly to a grieving, aching heart; or music that God used in a revival to communicate the gospel and prepare the hearts of the lost and indifferent to be open and responsive to the Holy Spirit's work? Have you seen God use music to gain a hearing for Christian witness in secular settings—shopping centers, auditoriums, parks, resorts, community or school events—reaching persons who rarely, if ever, enter a church building?

Think of music in the current life of your church. What is its role in communicating the gospel and building up the church?

Writing in the March 1986 *Church Musician,* Wesley Forbis, director of the Church Music Department of the Sunday School Board, described music's contribution to Bold Mission Thrust:

> Church musicians throughout the Southern Baptist Convention have joined hands to launch a plan so bold that it will forever change not only our lives, but the lives of those whom we touch and those yet to be born. It is based on the belief that minister-musicians, through the program of Music Ministry, can "Reach People," "Develop Believers," "Strengthen Missions." It is called "Musicians-on-Mission . . . That All May Hear" (1985-1990). It is predicated on the audacious commitment of Bold Mission Thrust that we [Southern Baptists] will have presented Christ to every human being by the year 2000 AD. Let no musician undervalue the implications of the theme or its power to bring life to the unborn living.
>
> Our first major challenge is to have 1990 by 1990 (that is, an enrollment of 1,990,000 [in the Music Ministries of Southern Baptist churches] by 1990). Some of us will have passed from the scene by then, but it will be these 1,990,000 who will carry the song into the last decade of this century.

The challenge to reach the goal will require (1) an increase in the number of approved workers; (2) an increase in the number of Journeyman music missionaries; (3) an increase in the teaching/training activities of local churches and associations; (4) an increase in musical witnessing projects; (5) an increase in local church, association, and state participation in new-work states, national as well as foreign mission stations.

The first step in achieving these increases will be regional Musicians on Mission Workshops. . . . Placed in strategic cities bordering established and new-work areas, they will be the catalyst for our success.[1]

This information illustrates the encouragement and support denominational programs are prepared to give churches in helping them be on bold mission.

What Is the Work of the Music Ministry?

The Music Ministry exists for every person in the church and as a method for reaching persons outside the church. It should improve the quality and use of music in all congregational worship services and activities of church program organizations. It should help every member of the church and its organizations understand the appropriateness, the meaning, and the significance of church music. The Music Ministry offers church members opportunities for service and Christian growth as they use their God-given talents in singing, playing instruments, and/or leading musical activities for others. It offers others opportunities to participate in praising God and witnessing to His grace through congregational and small-group singing.

The Music Ministry should involve church members in responsible discipleship which results in the use of their talent in the worship and service of the church. New members are easily assimilated into the fellowship of the church through involvement in music activities. Through music experiences some persons are led to a lifelong commitment to Jesus Christ and responsible church membership. Christian children, youth, and adults need to understand that they are part of the fellowship of believers—the body of

Christ, God's people. As members of the body, all Christian disciples have unique functions to fulfill. The Music Ministry is engaged in helping members discover their musical talents, develop those talents to the fullest potential, and use them to God's glory in helping His people be on bold mission in the world. As talents are developed and exercised, the spirit of the church is freshened; and the tempo of church growth is quickened.[2]

God's people in a church can look to the Music Ministry to accomplish five tasks that will help the church be on bold mission.

Task 1: Provide Musical Experiences in Congregational Services
Through this task the Music Ministry is most visible on a regular basis to the congregation and to visitors. It gives the Music Ministry responsibility for planning, rehearsing, arranging, performing, and leading music for all congregational services and for making available musical resources needed to achieve the desired outcomes for the services. The term *congregational services* includes Sunday morning and evening worship, prayer meeting, revival services, special services or events, and other gatherings intended for the entire membership or large groups of them.

The purpose of this task is to provide inspiration, instruction, and collective expression that enables all participants in congregational services to move toward a more perfect relationship with God and the Christian community. The only valid reason for the existence of the Music Ministry is that it aids in achieving the church's mission. The ministry of music in the congregational services fufills its purpose when it gives expression to and supports the church's functions of worship, proclamation and witness, and nurture and education.

Some of the media used to provide music are the congregation, large and small performing groups (vocal and instrumental), keyboard instruments, solos, and recorded music.

> Music is a means of worship. . . . Through music one may engage in praise, adoration, petition, intercession, confession, and repentance. The flights of imagination and feeling expressed through singing aid the worshiper to voice his feelings to God more clearly and more

satisfactorily than in other ways. Music is in no sense a substitute for prayer or for the personal expression of the worshiper in his own words and thought patterns. However, it is a mistake to think of music in the worship service as being incidental, perfunctory, or something to be engaged in while latecomers are being seated, while the offering is being received, or while the church is being properly ventilated. . . .

Christians bear a real witness through their singing. They sing of what Christ did to save them, and what he did to save all sinners. They sing of his death, burial, resurrection, and second coming. They proclaim his love, grace, and power to save. They express in song the glorious gospel and the joys of their own salvation. They testify through song.[3]

A wide variety of music can be used in accomplishing this task, but it should all be scripturally and doctrinally sound. It should also have musical and literary integrity and should fit the backgrounds and abilities as well as the cultural and aesthetic environment of the people in the congregation.

Music Ministry leaders, members, and sometimes the congregation itself will accomplish this task. The pastor should lead in planning and conducting congregational services, but the music director shares in that responsibility. Because music is such a large portion of many worship services, the music director may be asked to do the basic staff work in planning. Other staff colleagues and—ideally—members of the congregation may be enlisted to serve on a congregational services planning group.

In carrying out this task, music leaders will need to see that the following more specific essential actions are taken on a continuing basis:

1. Assist the pastor in planning the congregational services.

2. Lead in evaluating, selecting, creating, arranging, rehearsing, and performing music for congregational services.

3. Lead the congregation in musical experiences that are relevant, meaningful, inspiring, and that contribute to the thrust and mission of the church.

4. Motivate the church constituency to want to be involved in the musical experiences and to grow in their understanding of the

value and role of music in the congregational services.

5. Provide resources for musical experiences of the congregation.

Task 2: Provide Church Music Education

This tasks makes the Music Ministry responsible for planning and carrying out a definite schedule of teaching, training, and performing activities that are designed to (1) guide persons in developmental learning and performing experiences, (2) develop a positive attitude toward church music, and (3) increase knowledge and appreciation of the purposes and benefits of church music.

Development of musical skills helps persons to experience the presence of God and to realize more fully His indescribable mysteries. It also helps them lead others in similar experiences through musical involvement and expression. Church music education involves participants in musical growth and performance not only to help the individual find self-satisfaction, self-expression, and personal fulfillment but also to make provision for its people to become actively involved in the life of the church.

Target groups for music education include all church members, their families, and other prospects. The education may be offered through choirs, ensembles, and other continuing groups; short-term learning projects, such as study courses and Equipping Center modules; and performance projects, such as preparation of a musical drama, preparation for adjudication in a choir or handbell festival, or providing music as part of a missions project of the church or youth group.

Content for this task includes a curriculum with a balanced approach to music education and music performance, designed to meet the needs of the age group involved. The curriculum provides for sequential and holistic learning experiences through performance activities that are based on the mental, physical, and spiritual readinesses of individuals. Resources available from the Baptist Sunday School Board include leader and member age-graded periodicals; Church Study Course materials; BTN software; and Broadman, Van Ness, and McKinney music.

The Music Ministry in each church should design its own *schedule,* tailored to meet the needs of those involved. But all rehearsals and other meetings of the Music Ministry groups should be carefully coordinated through the Church Council to avoid conflict with other activities.

To ensure that this task is carried out effectively, Music Ministry leaders need to:

1. Discover and analyze the musical needs of the church constituency, that is, instructional programs, training, and performance.

2. Provide the instructional programs, training, and performance opportunities appropriate to those needs.

3. Motivate the church constituency to see the needs and to be involved in instructional programs, training, and performance activities.

Task 3: Lead the Church to Witness and Minister Through Music

The Music Ministry is responsible for leading persons to witness and minister through musical experiences and activites in the church and community. It uses the music resources of the church in actively seeking ways to witness and minister through music to believers and unbelievers.

Because music is such an incomparable and widely used means of communication, the Music Ministry is in a unique position to proclaim the message of redemption and to respond to the heart cry of a needy world. To fail to acknowledge that church music is not only a worship act within itself but is also a valuable method or tool would be to ignore one of God's greatest instruments of communication. As a means for communicating feelings, music can enrich and strengthen meanings communicated through words.

In accomplishing this task, music leaders need to:

1. Discover and analyze needs for musical witness and ministry.

2. Develop plans for individual and group involvement in musical witness and ministry.

3. Involve members in individual and group musical witness and ministry projects.

Much of the witnessing and ministry through music is done through the regular congregational services. Other opportunities are revivals, weddings, funerals, special occasions, music dramas and pageants, oratorios and cantatas, concerts and recitals, song sermons, and musicals.

Another approach is to assist other churches or missions through the loan or gift of music, recordings, and equipment and to let them share in a church's music leadership training events such as music schools, choir demonstrations, workshops, clinics, festivals, and lectures.

Individual and group musical talents can be used to minister to people with physical and/or spiritual needs in homes, nursing homes, and prisons. Participation by church musicians in community or institutional musical projects can open up numerous opportunities for witness and ministry.

Growing numbers of church members and leaders are using their musical talents in missions projects of various types locally, in other states, and in foreign countries. Musicians on Mission will increase opportunities for this kind of ministry, and church musicians should be encouraged to serve in this way.

The growing field of electronic mass media—videocassettes, radio broadcasts, televised services or special programs, Southern Baptists' ACTS network, and audio recording and tape ministry— has great potential for witness and ministry through music.

Churches that want to be on bold mission need to give this task greater attention than ever before. Musical programs in church buildings and in secular settings can reach persons who are not responsive to traditional services. Christian music provided over television and radio can communicate the gospel and stimulate the interest of persons who are not church related.

Teenagers and young adults in our society are strongly influenced by contemporary music. They are bombarded by secular, humanistic, sub-Christian—even flagrantly immoral and vulgar—sights, sounds, and values through broadcast and cable television, satellite reception directly into homes, music videos, audiocassettes, motion pictures in theatres and on home videocassettes, and radio.

God's people need to turn the power of these media to the service of God in communicating the Christian gospel and Christian lifestyle. This will involve taking full advantage of couching the gospel in music styles that will gain the attention of children, youth, and young adults in today's culture. The Bible speaks in numerous references of using all kinds of instruments in the praise and service of the Lord. Nowhere does it say that only traditional styles of Christian music which may rest easiest on the ears of older Christians are to be used by God's people in reaching the lost for Him. Some of us may have a tendency to think that any Christian music which differs in style from what we "grew up on" or prefer is not suitable or worthy for church use in worship or in outreach. With regard to the music and media we use to communicate the gospel in our contemporary culture, we must be careful to avoid being hindered in our God-given mission by our own "traditions," as the Pharisees were in Jesus' day.

Music Ministry activities that provide opportunities for evangelism should be planned in relationship to the church's comprehensive strategy of evangelism, as discussed in chapter 9.

Task 4: Assist Church Programs in Providing Training in Music Skills and in Consultation About Music Equipment

This task places the Music Ministry at the service of those church programs whose leaders want to use music to enrich their work. Because music is specialized in several areas (singing, playing instruments, song leading), the church's music director may be looked upon as a developer of skills in these areas. He or she is also a resource person for information and advice about other music needs, such as hymnals, keyboard instruments, graded choir instruments, or sound equipment. On request of a program leader, the music director will confer about the needs of the program and supply needed training or consultation in cooperation with the program leader.

All such plans for needed skill development activities for new leaders or existing leaders will be coordinated through the Church Council before the training is conducted. After plans are coordinated and approved, the music director will provide the training in cooperation with the leaders of the programs whose workers are involved in the training.

Music development activities for leaders in other programs can be accomplished before the singer, song leader, or accompanist begins service, or they can be "on the job" in nature for teachers and leaders who need to improve their skills in using music in their teaching or the other activities for which they are responsible. Short-term class or group sessions, ongoing class sessions, or private instruction are ways the Music Ministry can provide the needed training in music skills.

The Music Ministry may also provide training that will be of interest to church members generally, as well as to leaders in programs. For example, the Music Ministry and Church Training programs of my church recently provided at Church Training time the Equipping Center module *Growing in Worship—Hymns,* with the Music Ministry providing the leader.

Task 5: Interpret and Undergird the Work of the Church and the Denomination

The Music Ministry shares this important task with all other basic church programs. Music Ministry leaders will take initiative to share information about the activities of the church and the denomination with persons in the program's activities. The intended message will be presented and explained in a manner appropriate for Music Ministry tasks.

Music Ministry leaders and groups provide support for the work of other programs and for congregational projects of all types such as weeks of prayer for missions, revivals, and church picnics.

To illustrate, when Judson Baptist Church in Nashville recently celebrated its seventy-fifth anniversary in a month-long series of events, the sanctuary choir was heavily involved in supporting the celebration by providing special music for worship and the music for two dramas about the mission of the church as the people of God. But beyond that, the minister of music kept the choir informed about other aspects of the celebration and strongly encouraged their participation in other celebration events.

In support of the Week of Prayer for Foreign Missions and the Lottie Moon Christmas Offering, young adults in the Music Ministry presented the musical drama *Lottie D.* The Music Ministry worked through the Church Council to agree on responsibilities for these events.

The Potential of Music for Bold Mission Thrust

These lines from *A Church on Mission*, published in 1980, continue to be timely and descriptive of the potential contribution music can make to a church on bold mission.

"The music heard in the churches has experienced as much change in recent years as any area of the church's life. . . . However strange and unsettling the sights and sounds may be to those who don't like change, we need to understand that this is not the first time such events have occurred in Christian song. Neither will it be the last. To be able to harness the vitality and strength of church music in this day and to use it in the church's mission, boldly and skillfully, is a challenge that demands our best."[4]

Writing in the *Church Musician*, Wesley Forbis summarized his belief about the place of music in a church: "I believe that every church musician must have a mission greater than that of music making and that the purpose of that mission is to be on mission in *theology, history, education, aesthetics, evangelism*."[5]

✎ ::

Pause and Do: *Personal Learning Activity 12*
1. Describe briefly what church music contributes to your Christian life.
2. Which of the Music Ministry tasks is (are) most effectively carried on in your church? Explain briefly why you selected the one(s) you did.
3. List three ways your church might use music in witness and ministry (ways not now being used).

::: ⌨

---

[1]Wesley Forbis, "The Ministry of Song," *Church Musician*, March 1986, p. 42.
[2]Adapted from Reginald M. McDonough, comp., *A Church on Mission: an Intentional Response to the Needs of the Eighties* (Nashville: Convention Press, 1980), p. 138.
[3]W. L. Howse and W. O. Thomason, *A Church Organized and Functioning* (Nashville: Convention Press, 1963), pp. 112-13.
[4]McDonough, p. 141.
[5]Wesley Forbis, "Editorial," *Church Musician*, September 1986, p. 42.

CHAPTER 8

Sharing God's Love Through Missions

Christ's commission has echoed through the centuries, transcending time and outliving all eras. The commission is contemporary: "Go, then, to all peoples everywhere and make them my disciples: baptize them in the name of the Father and of the Son and of the Holy Spirit, and teach them to obey everything I have commanded you. And remember! I will be with you always, to the end of the age" (Matt. 28:19-20, TEV). . . .

Christ's commission is a mandate with a world scope—all nations, even unto the end of the world. The mission he describes is the most demanding assignment ever made. Christ, who commissioned his church and gave his followers their marching orders, describes his work in the world in clear terms. The contemporary challenge is as exacting as the original one: a church must be able to take hold of its mission on Christ's scale—giving the whole gospel to the whole world.[1]

By committing ourselves to Bold Mission Thrust—the effort to reach every person on earth with the gospel by the year 2000—we Southern Baptists are focusing our energies and our commitment on this commission of the Lord.

Leaders of Southern Baptist Convention agencies have defined *missions* as "what churches do in keeping with the commission of their sovereign Lord to extend their witness and ministry beyond themselves to bring all persons to Christ and to glorify God."[2] In line with that meaning, the Southern Baptist Convention has adopted "Strengthen Missions" as one of the three major goal areas in Bold Mission Thrust through 1990.

The missions programs to be discussed in this chapter, the basic programs of Woman's Missionary Union and Brotherhood and the emphasis program of Missions Development, by task assignment can accomplish important work related to this goal area for a church. No matter how many strong slogans and goals are developed, missions will be strengthened only as God's people in the churches commit themselves to greater involvement in the bold mission Christ has given them.

Missions—Woman's Missionary Union

Carolyn Weatherford, executive director of Woman's Missionary Union, has described the purpose of the program in these words:

The very name of Woman's Missionary Union defines its purpose—missions. In a church, Woman's Missionary Union is known as a missions organization. Since the beginning of Woman's Missionary Union in 1888, its purpose has been to promote Christian missions through a program of mission study, mission action, and mission support.

Because every church of God's people has a missions responsibility which includes teaching missions, praying for missions, giving for the support of missions, and ministering and witnessing to lost persons, Woman's Missionary Union exists to help a church accomplish these tasks in fulfilling its missions responsibility.

Through the organization of Woman's Missionary Union, church members become aware of and are equipped to respond to the mission of the church beyond its immediate witness—to the ends of the

earth. . . . Church members will never be deeply involved in missions
apart from a regular program of missions education.[3]

The Tasks of Woman's Missionary Union

Woman's Missionary Union is designed to accomplish four tasks
for a church. Each of these is briefly described in the paragraphs
which follow.

Task 1: Teach Missions

The teaching of missions is a vitally important part of the total
education program of a Southern Baptist church. An understanding
of and commitment to missions is vital to the health and usefulness
of a church. Missions is a church's way of showing that God's people are concerned for all people everywhere and are willing to suffer
with them in confronting the problems which make it difficult for
them to establish a relationship with God.

In teaching missions WMU stimulates and guides persons in
learning experiences that bring personal growth in knowledge, understanding, appreciations, attitudes, and skills. Learners are led to
explore with growing understanding the nature, implications, and
evidences of God's missionary purpose and to respond to that purpose in personal commitment and obedience. Teaching missions
helps the church to become concerned and to express that concern
through praying, giving, ministering to missionaries and their families, witnessing, participating in mission action, providing an environment for persons to respond to God's call to mission service
and nurturing those who respond, and volunteering for mission service.

Content for teaching missions includes the biblical basis of Christian missions, the progress of Chistian missions, contemporary missions, and spiritual development of the learner as related to
missions. Missions as defined earlier in this chapter is divided into
two parts—direct missions and representative missions. Direct missions is a church's direct and personal involvement in missions.
Representative missions is missions work that a church cannot do

alone and therefore does in cooperation with other churches through the association, state convention, and Southern Baptist Convention.

At all age levels a large proportion of the study time is given to contemporary missions. Members need to know what the mission boards and the state conventions are doing in fulfilling their obligation to the churches that have established them and support their efforts to do representative mission work for the churches.

The spiritual development of the learner is a significant part of teaching missions. Each member of a WMU organization is led to discover the meaning of prayer, personal meditation, stewardship, mission action and personal witnessing, and career and noncareer mission service.

Most of the teaching of missions is done through age-level organizations for women, girls, and preschoolers. In addition, special study projects are promoted for individuals, families, and the entire church.

Through the study of missions, God's work in the world is personalized in the life of the member in such a way that she may feel a heightened desire to become involved in missions. The next two tasks provide opportunities to express actively the concern developed through study.

Task 2: Engage in Mission Action and Personal Witnessing
This task includes two types of action that are required of God's people who take seriously their God-given mission—mission action and personal witnessing.

Mission action means ministering and witnessing to persons of special need or circumstance who are not members of the church or its programs.—It includes combating social and moral problems. For preschoolers it means helping others.

Mission action is the here-and-now expression of a church's belief that all persons need God and must come to Him through Christ and that a church must demonstrate concern for persons outside its membership.

Through engaging in mission action, God's people are faithful to the command and example of Christ. They are helping the church to become and to be known as a ministering and witnessing body. Being God's people in the fullest sense involves in-depth commitment to mission action.

Mission action may be focused on both the needs of special groups and on social and moral problems that victimize persons. The action taken may be preventive, remedial, or both.

Some of the special groups that may need mission action are prisoners, juvenile delinquents, alcoholics, drug abusers, migrants, military personnel, latch-key kids, the poor, language groups, internationals, nonreaders, the aging, unwed parents, the sick, the abused, minority groups, and the institutionalized.

Mission action designed to meet needs of one of these groups always includes both ministering and witnessing. The type of ministry and the method of witnessing are determined by the special needs and circumstances of the recipients and the length of time involved. For example, when contact with persons in a target group is limited, witnessing efforts may be limited to giving the recipient a Scripture portion. Persons in these groups need special attention from a church because a church's usual approaches for reaching prospects may miss them.

Some of the issues toward which mission action may need to be directed are family problems, gambling, pornography, obscenity, alcoholism, drug abuse, racial problems, economic problems, and political problems.

Personal witnessing is a Christian's sharing the gospel of Jesus Christ with another person and giving him or her an opportunity to confess Jesus Christ as Savior and Lord.—It also includes distributing Scripture. Doubtless almost any active Southern Baptist has a good general idea of what personal witnessing means. But the words in this task that need even more of our attention are *"engage in"*—meaning to become involved in or to begin and carry on a certain type of activity. Our Lord did not instruct us just to know what personal witnessing means or just to talk about it; He instructed us to be witnesses—to *engage in personal witnessing.* Being God's people means being His witnesses in word and in deed. Nothing else we do at the church building or for the church can substitute for personal witnessing.

Any person who is not a Christian needs personal witnessing, but the primary concern in WMU is reaching persons who are not members of a church program organization.

The content of personal witnessing includes the facts of gospel history—God's creation and original intention for mankind, sin and its results, God's provision of redemption culminating in Christ, and how a person may restore the God-human fellowship by accepting through repentance and faith in what Christ has done and placing his or her life back under God's control. Personal witnessing also includes personal testimony about God's actions in the life of the witness and whatever additional understandings the person receiving the witness needs in order to apply the gospel to his or her own life, to make it personally meaningful.

WMU leads Christian members of its organizations to witness in two ways: by individuals for individuals and by groups for individuals and/or groups of persons. Both ways may be sponsored by a WMU organization, or WMU may encourage its members to participate in witnessing efforts sponsored by other church programs. WMU witnessing efforts are planned in relation to the church's comprehensive strategy of evangelism discussed in chapter 9.

Task 3: Support Missions

In this task, *"missions"* refers to the representative missions work being conducted for churches by representative missions programs in the association, state convention, and Southern Baptist Convention (associational missions, state missions, home missions, and foreign missions).

WMU leads members of its organizations and other church members to become involved in various activities that support missions including:

Praying for missions is communication with God in behalf of missionaries and missions work. Prayer and missions are inseparably linked. Churches need to help their members become aware of the potential of prayer. Praying for missions is one way persons can "go into all the world."

Giving to missions provides financial support for representative missions work. Persons are encouraged to give through the local church. Tithing, giving through the Cooperative Program, and giving to special offerings such as the state mission offering, the Lottie Moon Christmas Offering for Foreign Missions, and the Annie Armstrong Easter Offering for Home Missions are emphasized.

Providing personal ministries for missionaries and their families includes words of encouragement and acts of human kindness, such as writing letters, making calls, caring for children and parents, making transportation and housing available, and providing other needed ministries.

Emphasizing the need for persons to become involved in mission service includes helping to create an environment in which persons can hear and respond to God's call to mission service.

Nurturing the persons who respond to God's call to mission service includes providing support, information, and encouragement to help them follow God's leadership into mission service.

Being involved in volunteer mission service is participating in mission projects in support of missions work being conducted by association, state convention, Home Mission Board, and Foreign Mission Board.

This task helps link God's people in a church with missions efforts around the world.

Task 4: Interpret and Undergird the Work of the Church and the Denomination

Woman's Missionary Union shares this task with all other basic church programs. It gives WMU responsibility for making church members and their families aware of the work of the church and the denomination. Through the organizations and activities WMU leads, information is communicated and explained so that persons can understand it sufficiently to relate appropriately to the work and to participate meaningfully in it.

The leaders of WMU organizations in a church take primary responsibility for accomplishing this task. They work closely with the pastor, staff, and leaders of other church programs to help the church fulfill its God-given mission in a coordinated, effective manner.

Missions—Brotherhood

Involving men and boys in missions is one of the greatest challenges and opportunities facing Southern Baptist churches as they work to make Bold Mission Thrust a reality. Growing numbers of Southern Baptist men and boys are being challenged by the spiritual and physical needs of people throughout the world. They are responding to the challenge by becoming involved in various types of missions activities and ministry projects in their communities and in other parts of the nation and world. There is growing participation in lay evangelism, disaster relief, renewal, and mission work by men and boys in the churches. Seeing and meeting these opportunities depends on the vision, the depth of concern, and the degree of commitment of Southern Baptist pastors, men, and boys.[4]

With those words in mind, consider this expression of testimony and conviction from James H. Smith, president of the Southern Baptist Brotherhood Commission:

> Two weeks before I was affirmed as president of the Commission, God gave me a word of assurance from Psalm 110:3. God said to me that in the day of His power, His people would volunteer as a mighty army. As they march forth in holy array, it will be the dawning of a new day. That day has come upon us. Volunteerism is one of the most exciting dimensions of our present missionary enterprise.
>
> The Brotherhood Commission is committed to helping churches involve men and boys in missions. It is God's will and purpose that the whole world be evangelized. It can only be accomplished as a greater task force is mobilized.[5]

The purpose of Brotherhood is to help a church involve men and boys in missions. This purpose is expressed in missions activities, mission study, mission support, and personal ministry. Brotherhood seeks to develop a fellowship of believers bound together in Christian love and common purpose, giving men and boys opportunity for ministry to others and involvement in missions-evangelism. Involvement in missions is men and boys living their faith, having personal experiences in witness and ministry, and giving and praying to support persons involved in missions.

The Tasks of Brotherhood

Brotherhood helps a church be on bold mission by involving men and boys in five church tasks similar to those of Woman's Missionary Union.

Task 1: Engage in Missions Activities
Brotherhood seeks to involve men and boys in both ministry and a learning environment. The term *"missions activities"* includes mission action, personal evangelism, mass evangelism, and special missions projects.

Mission action means "ministering and witnessing to persons of special need or circumstances who are not members of the church or its programs." It also includes efforts to combat social and moral problems. Examples of special groups that need ministry and witness and of problems that need to be addressed were given in the preceding section.

Personal evangelism is a Christian sharing the gospel of Jesus Christ with another person or persons under the guidance of the Holy Spirit to lead them to a confession of Jesus Christ as Savior and Lord. Lay-led revivals, lay-renewal efforts, and prison ministry can provide both motivation and special opportunities for personal evangelism.

Mass evangelism is the church proclaiming the gospel to its community in special events, projects, and activities. Brotherhood can work through its organizations to involve men and boys in carrying out significant, specific responsibilities related to such mass evangelism efforts.

Special missions projects are organized efforts to witness and minister to persons within and beyond the association through a variety of projects such as Scripture distribution; disaster relief in the community, in other states, or in foreign countries; the erection or renovation of church buildings; or survey work and mission Vacation Bible School work in pioneer areas, perhaps through the state convention partnership relationship.

Brotherhood witnessing efforts are planned in relation to the church's comprehensive strategy of evangelism discussed in chapter 9.

Task 2: Teach Missions

Brotherhood teaches missions to men and boys in order to lay the foundation for them to grow in closeness to Christ and to respond to the Great Commission. Men and boys need to know what God is doing throughout the world and how they fit into His plan of redemption. God's work is personalized through missions.

Some of the learning experiences occur in structured classroom situations; others happen in informal situations and through involvement in missions activities.

Brotherhood organizations teach men and boys the missionary message of the Bible, the progress of Christian missions, and contemporary missions, with an emphasis on contemporary missions. The emphasis on teaching contemporary missions is on local church support of representative mission work through prayer, giving, and personnel, with special attention to building an awareness of the need for career and short-term missions personnel.

The teaching is done through Baptist Men and Royal Ambassador organizations and may take place in church buildings, homes, retreats, assembly conferences, and in connection with involvement in various types of missions activities.

Brotherhood teaches missions to men and boys in order to lay the foundation for them to grow in closeness to Christ and to respond to the Great Commission. It is not enough to know what God is doing in the church and community. Church members, and especially men and boys, need to know what He is doing throughout the world and how they fit into His plan of redemption.

Tasks 3: Pray for and Give to Missions

Missions as defined earlier in this chapter involves God's people in efforts to achieve their mission in areas of human need which are on the growing edge of the church's confrontation with the non-Christian world. Prayer and giving are two of the major types of support the missions effort needs.

Our Lord taught us to pray the Lord of the harvest to send forth laborers; and He set the example of praying for missions by praying for those whom He sent into the world, both during His earthly life and in all the ages to come (see John 17). He prayed for us and all the missionaries we support. By communicating with God in behalf of missions work and the persons involved in it, God's people bring the power of God to bear on missions efforts and acknowledge that His power is required to make missions effective.

By fervent prayer for missions, the Christian who does not feel called to go can show concern for the lost and invest his or her life in the worldwide missions work of those who are called. Through the prayer experience comes the sweet blessing of a growing relationship with God.

Giving to missions means to provide material resources, especially money, to be used in support of missions. Through its organizations Brotherhood strongly emphasizes giving through the Cooperative Program of Southern Baptists in support of missions. It also cooperates with Woman's Missionary Union in promoting the major special offerings for missions—the Lottie Moon Christmas Offering for Foreign Missions, the Annie Armstrong Easter Offering for Home Missions, and offerings for state missions. Brotherhood encourages men and boys to give generously as one way to participate in fulfilling a church's mission.

Task 4: Develop Personal Ministry

This task rests on the concept that each Christian has a call to ministry and that God has provided gifts for fulfilling that ministry. Each Christian needs to discover and utilize his gifts "for the work of Christian service, in order to build up the body of Christ" (Eph. 4:12, GNB).

This task focuses on developing spiritual gifts of participants in Brotherhood organizations by directing them toward ministry, especially through engaging in missions activities, teaching missions, and praying for and giving to missions. Primary initative in a church for the process of discovering gifts rests with Church Training. Brotherhood's responsibility is supportive and channeled through its approach to missions. Understanding of self and of ministry comes as a consequence of other Brotherhood tasks and exists as a meaningful goal of missions education and accomplishment.

A part of each Christian's ministry is to encourage and support other Christians who are in the process of developing their personal ministry. It is important to encourage church leaders such as pastor, staff, deacons, and church-elected leaders in programs in their ministry of equipping others.

Task 5: Interpret and Undergird the Work of the Church and the Denomination

Brotherhood shares this task with WMU and all other basic church programs. Brotherhood leaders use its organizations, activities, and materials to help members of the organizations understand and support the work of the church and the denomination. In doing this they must secure or receive the information to be communicated, communicate it to the audiences that need it, and evaluate the understandings and involvement achieved. Effective accomplishment of this task should enable persons to participate more meaningfully in bold mission activities of the church, association, state convention, and Southern Baptist Convention.

At the request of the church, the Brotherhood may also undergird its work by providing organization and leadership for special projects and ministries. Examples of these include lay-renewal events, missions visitation, stewardship, enlistment, new-church types of missions work, transportation, and work projects.

‍‍

Pause and Do: *Personal Learning Activity 13*
1. What is the total enrollment of Woman's Missionary Union and Brotherhood in your church? Add the two enrollments and compare the total to the total resident membership of your church.
2. Find out what percentage of your church's total budget offerings goes to missions.
3. What do the answers to questions 1 and 2 suggest to you about the priority God's people in your church give to missions education, direct involvement, and support?

‍‍

Missions—Missions Development Program

The Missions Development program in a church is a newly developed emphasis program. It replaces and incorporates the previous emphasis program Starting New Churches. The Missions Development program can help churches place more emphasis on direct missions than ever before.

In commenting on the rationale and background for Missions Development in a church, J. B. Graham, assistant vice-president for missions at the Home Mission Board has written these words:

> The church is God's primary agency for missions. . . . The church's mission is the same as that of her Lord. It is the carrying out of the mission of Christ Himself. "As my Father hath sent me, even so send I you" (John 20:21).
>
> The mission of the church then is to make Jesus Christ known by addressing new frontiers of need and opportunity, presenting the gospel to all the people of the world with the purpose of leading them to personal faith in Christ and obedience to His will.
>
> Churches across the Southern Baptist Convention (SBC) have always been sensitive to missions. . . . In the forties and fifties, churches began to organize into "committees" to do hands-on missions in their cities, feeling that financial support alone was not enough. . . .
>
> With the coming of Bold Mission Thrust, state-to-state partnerships, and increasing volunteerism, Baptists are even more anxious to do hands-on missions in the local church. Church Missions Development is the newer concept and parallels the associational Missions Development program, which provides a channel of resourcing and training.[6]

Missions Development emphasis program in a church actively seeks to discover missions opportunities and needs and to work with church organizations or individuals to respond appropriately to those needs. It recognizes that the Woman's Missionary Union and Brotherhood carry primary responsibility for missions education and support and for conducting mission action projects in response to discovered needs. It works closely with all church programs to implement its tasks and to make maximum impact for missions concerns through all available channels, especially basic programs. Its tasks reflect the duties that in the past have been carried by the church missions committee.

The Missions Development program will help a church be sensitive to the following missions concerns: unreached geographical areas, racial groups, socioeconomic needs, ethnic/cultural groups, institutional concerns, religious/philosophical groups, and lifestyle. WMU and Brotherhood work with Missions Development in helping a church be sensitive to missions concerns.

The Tasks of Missions Development

A well-organized and functioning emphasis program of Missions Development can lead in accomplishing four important church tasks.

Task 1: Identify Missions Needs/Opportunities

More needs exist in every community than any church can adequately meet. Missions Development has primary responsibility for gathering information about missions needs and opportunities which the congregation and WMU and Brotherhood can use in deciding which missions needs can best be addressed with available resources.

Through in-church and community surveys, reading, interviews, field experience, associational and governmental survey reports, and other specialized sources of information, Missions Development can conduct an ongoing survey of missions needs and opportunities in the community and the association. These efforts will be carried on in close cooperation with the leaders of other church programs and especially with WMU, Brotherhood, and Sunday School that have survey responsibilities related to their tasks.

Missions Development encourages church members to be aware of and to share missions concerns. It inventories human and financial resources available in the church, community, association, state convention, and denominational agencies. It shares information with persons or groups in the church to heighten concern for persons who need the missions response of the church. The primary focus of this task is in the church's community, but it may also include cooperative endeavors in the association.

Task 2: Develop Missions Strategies to Respond to Unmet Missions Needs

Missions Development leads in preparing plans for using available resources to meet missions needs not being addressed by any other church program. Missions Development program leaders, including WMU and Brotherhood representatives, who review the missions needs and opportunities, determine which needs are currently being met adequately and agree on responsibility for strategies to respond to unmet needs. Proposed strategies will be taken to the Church Council for further development and coordination before presentation to the church for approval according to church policy.

Many projects by nature, assignment, and/or tradition are the responsiblity of Brotherhood and WMU, either independently or jointly. As unmet needs are identified, Missions Development leaders will encourage and assist programs to accept appropriate projects for implementation. For strategies not accepted by other programs, Missions Development leaders will be responsible for establishing project teams and enlisting leaders, with approval according to church policy.

Task 3: Establish New Churches

In Bold Mission Thrust Goal Area I, "Reach People," Southern Baptists have commited themselves to a goal of starting five thousand new churches by September 30, 1990. A similar goal will likely be developed for 1990-95 and beyond. "The cutting edge—the point of thrust—in missions is church planting. Ministry, education, and training follow the birth of a church. . . . To be involved in church planting today is to be at the very heart of missions."[7]

This task (previously a responsibility of the missions committee) makes the Missions Development program responsible for leading the church to establish new churches. *Church* in this task means "any ongoing congregational group of believers." The group may begin as a Bible study fellowship, a mission Sunday School, a preaching point, or through a mission action project by WMU or Brotherhood.

Missions Development leaders work to create a climate for new churches and to identify needs for new congregations. They help the church be aware of factors within its community that relate to the need for new churches, such as housing patterns; age changes; the presence of language, cultural, religious, and ethnic groups; and family patterns. Inner-city areas need to be seen as opportunities for establishing new churches. Establishing a new church may be the best way to minister to language, cultural, religious, and ethnic groups in some situations.

The immediate church field should have first priority when identifying unchurched groups and beginning new work. Any involvement beyond the local church field should be coordinated with appropriate associational leaders.

Though the Missions Development program leaders have primary responsibility for this task, other church programs will relate to the effort in line with their tasks as developing plans are coordinated through the Church Council and approved by the church.

With church approval, leaders of the Missions Development program (now called the Missions Development Council when they meet together for planning and coordination) develop necessary plans for any needed survey work and new church field cultivation and initiate preliminary activities. They work cooperatively with other church programs in approaches such as new Sunday Schools, Bible study fellowships, Backyard Bible Clubs, mission Vacation Bible Schools, literacy classes, Big A Clubs, and student ministry projects.

Task 4: Support Establishing and Strengthening WMU and Brotherhood

This task commits the church Missions Development emphasis program to assist actively in the initiation, promotion, and utilization of Woman's Missionary Union and Brotherhood because these programs have a primary role in developing persons who are sensitive to and motivated toward significant direct missions involvement. Without active missions education and awareness in a church, the ability to do missions is weakened.

If a church does not have WMU or Brotherhood, Missions Development leaders can work with pastor and/or appropriate church staff, associational leaders, and state convention leaders to encourage establishing the missing program(s). In small or new churches, either of these programs can be started by finding a person who has a commitment to missions and a willingness to work and enlisting him or her to lead a project in the areas of WMU or Brotherhood tasks, such as the week of prayer for home or foreign missions. As additional interest is stimulated and more leaders become available, the program can grow by doing additional projects or by beginning one or more WMU and/or Brotherhood organizations.

Missions Development leaders can give support by praying for existing WMU and Brotherhood work and for the starting of needed new work, cooperating with WMU and Brotherhood leaders in the accomplishment of missions emphases and projects, and including a representative from the programs on the Missions Development Council to participate in effective coordination of the church's missions plans.

All plans for Missions Development activities are coordinated with other church program plans through the Church Council in order to achieve maximum involvement of other programs as appropriate for their tasks and to avoid duplication of effort and conflict in scheduling.

Leaders for Missions Development

Missions Development leaders selected and elected according to church policy are responsible to the church for implementing these tasks. The size of the organization for Missions Development is determined by the church as it relates to its strength and the needs in its community. Recommended officers are a director, missions survey director, WMU representative, and Brotherhood representative, plus project leaders as needed and approved by the church. In small situations, one person may have to carry the duties of two or more officers.

"The church Missions Development leaders working individually as per their job descriptions will bring information back periodically into a huddle that we call a council [Missions Development Council]. They will form strategies there and after coordination of plans through the Church Council and church approval will lead in actions to meet missions needs."[8]

This Missions Development Council is recommended as a replacement for the missions committee that has been recommended in the past. Another recommended change is that Missions Development leaders be elected (or reelected) annually as other program leaders are. The three-year rotation system is not recommended for these leaders so that continuation in office can allow them to benefit from training and experience.

The missions programs presented in this chapter are designed to enable a church to give high priority to involving God's people in missions education, support of home and foreign missions, and participation in the establishment of new churches and other direct missions efforts. These activities must become significantly higher priorities in most Southern Baptist churches if Bold Mission Thrust is to succeed. Is your church advancing or losing ground in missions? Are God's people gathered in your church ready to be a dynamic force in Bold Mission Thrust?

:::

Pause and Do: *Personal Learning Activity 14*
Answer these questions in your own words, after praying about their application to your church and your life.

1. In what sense are church members being God's people if they lack a personal, active commitment to extending their witness and ministry beyond themselves to bring all persons to Christ and glorify God (missions)?

2. Are you willing to let God change your priorities, your life-style, and your leadership if necessary for Him to work through you to help your church shape its life and work according to His priorities—to be on bold mission with Him? Note: A written answer to this question is not required for individual study credit or makeup work.

:::

---

[1]W. L. House and W. O. Thomason, *A Dynamic Church: Spirit and Structure for the Seventies* (Nashville: Convention Press, 1969), p. 68.

[2]"SBC Inter-Agency Glossary" (Prepared by the Coordinating Committee. Inter-Agency Council, SBC), p. 4.

[3]Carolyn Weatherford, executive director, Woman's Missionary Union, from resource material prepared for this book.

[4]Adapted from *Brotherhood Means Missions* (Memphis: Brotherhood Commission, SBC, 1984), p. 3.

[5]James A. Smith, president, Brotherhood Commission, SBC, from resource material prepared for this book.

[6]J. B. Graham, from material prepared for this book.

[7]Reginald M. McDonough, comp., *A Church on Mission: an Intentional Response to the Needs of the Eighties* (Nashville: Convention Press, 1980), p. 124.

[8]Graham.

CHAPTER 9

Reaching Persons for Christ

Can you think of a briefer or more biblical statement of the mission of God's people—of a church—than the title of this chapter—"Reaching Persons for Christ"? Can you think of any activity that is more fundamental to the success of Southern Baptists' Bold Mission Thrust to give every person in the world the opportunity to hear and accept the gospel by AD 2000?

Concerning the fundamental importance of reaching persons for Christ, Robert Hamblin, vice-president for evangelism at the Home Mission Board has said:

Since Jesus commissioned the church to make disciples and empowered the church with the Holy Spirit, its chief task has been to reach people. It is necessary to understand that Christ meant for people to be reached for salvation. It was His desire that all persons be forgiven of their sins by His own shed blood. The church must make its number one priority reaching people. In order for people to be reached, they must hear the Good News that Christ died for them, that He was buried and raised again. They must also be invited to receive Christ by a person or persons who care for them in the love of Christ. Each local church should plan a strategy which makes it possible for every person living in the community of the church to hear the message of Christ. The church must be evangelistic. To be evangelistic a church must plan a strategy for reaching the lost and depend on God for His power so that the church might be effective.[1]

Reaching Persons for Christ Through Church Programs

Because reaching persons for Christ—evangelism—is so basic to the mission of God's people and to any Southern Baptist church that intends to be on bold mission, evangelism must permeate the work of all church programs, as appropriate for their tasks.

The six basic programs each have tasks that give them specific responsibilities in reaching persons for Christ and other tasks that relate in a supportive way to evangelism.

The emphasis program of evangelism is designed to assist a church in developing a comprehensive strategy of evangelism in which plans for evangelistic efforts of all church programs are brought together through the Church Council into one churchwide plan for maximum evangelistic impact. In addition, it has responsibility for involving church members in personal evangelism and for using special events and mass evangelism in cooperation with other church programs to present the gospel of Christ.

Evangelism Through Basic Church Programs

Several tasks of the basic church programs are intended to involve God's people in sharing the gospel directly with those who need to hear it. Look back at the lists of tasks in chapter 3 and identify basic program tasks you think relate most obviously and directly to reaching the lost for Christ. Note which program has each task. Then compare your list with the following list.

Pastoral Ministries
• Proclaim the gospel to believers and unbelievers.

Bible Teaching
• Reach persons for Bible study.
• Witness to persons about Christ and lead persons into church membership.
• Minister to persons in need. (Ministry provides opportunity for verbal witnessing supported by demonstrated love and concern.)

Church Training
• Equip church members for discipleship and personal ministry. (Discipleship includes witnessing.)

Music Ministry
• Lead the church to witness and minister through music.

Brotherhood
• Engage in missions activities.
• Develop personal ministry. (Personal ministry provides opportunity for witnessing.)

Woman's Missionary Union
• Engage in mission action and personal witnessing. (WMU encourages training for witnessing and offers opportunities for witnessing.)

In addition to these tasks, several other tasks of basic programs relate less directly to evangelism.

As the pastor and other leaders of pastoral ministries lead the church in the accomplishment of its mission, they can help the church make reaching persons for Christ a top priority. They can also help create an evangelistic atmosphere throughout church life and can give leadership support to the evangelism program task of developing a comprehensive church strategy of evangelism and the other evangelism tasks. As they care for church members and other persons in the community, they will have opportunities to witness to lost persons in church families and to others.

Bible teaching should always be focused on reaching persons for Christ. Emphasizing the importance of the Sunday School in evangelism, Harry Piland, director of the Sunday School Department, Sunday School Board, wrote in 'Til Millions Know:

> For many years, teachers in Southern Baptist Sunday Schools have taught with an evangelistic purpose and goal. . . . Down through the years, Southern Baptist Sunday School leaders have rung out a loud call to use the Sunday School for evangelism. . . . Evangelism has not been the only purpose of the Sunday School, but it always has been a major purpose. It was clear and accepted. . . .
>
> But something has happened as the years have passed. The evangelistic spirit has not burned as brightly at times in many of our churches. Many Sunday Schools have not maintained a priority on evangelism. It is not uncommon to find large classes and departments without one unsaved person enrolled. Even in the midst of growth in our denomination, there does not seem to be a significant return to the priority of teaching to evangelize. This trend must be reversed. In this case, at least, we must go back to the basics. Every Sunday School should be evangelistic. . . .
>
> I am pleading for a priority on evangelism and for concern for lost persons in all teaching. I am pleading that every Sunday School worker see his or her role in the evangelistic mission of the church and take every opportunity to exercise that role.[2]

Church Training's tasks of reaching persons for discipleship training, orienting new church members for responsible church membership; teaching doctrine, ethics, Christian history, and church polity; and training church leaders for ministry can all emphasize equipping church members and leaders to be active and effective in personal evangelism.

The "teach missions" tasks give WMU and Brotherhood many fine opportunities to motivate the members to witness through both structured activities and life-style witnessing.

The task of interpreting and undergirding the work of the church and denomination, as shared by all basic programs, can be used with great effect to build a climate for evangelism and to inform members about available opportunities to train for and to participate in church and denominational efforts to reach the lost for Christ.

In some churches evangelism-related tasks of the basic church programs may be likened to seldom-used tools waiting to be put to their intended use. The pastor, staff, deacons, evangelism program leaders, and workers in other church programs who have a clear vision of what God expects of His people and are committed to leading the church to be evangelistic can put these tools to good use in the church's bold mission to change the quality of earthly life and the eternal destiny of those who need Christ.

Evangelism—an Emphasis Program

Evangelism is the presentation of the gospel of Christ in the power of the Holy Spirit in order to bring lost people to repentance and faith, to a commitment to Jesus as Lord and Savior, and to bring them into the fellowship of a local church where they will be able to become spiritually mature and will be witnesses of the gospel to other people.[3]

"This means more than living a good life and telling people about Jesus. Evangelism means to present verbally the gospel of Christ in the power of the Holy Spirit and to request the persons to repent of sin and receive Jesus Christ as Lord and Savior."[4] Evangelism is essential for a church that is determined to be the people of God on bold mission.

The evangelism emphasis program, with newly expanded tasks and a different organization, is designed to assist a church in developing and implementing an effective strategy for sharing the gospel with all persons, using the message, methods, motivation, and the spirit of New Testament evangelism. Because of its nature and importance as an emphasis program, evangelism depends heavily on other programs, especially basic programs, to provide education and information about evangelism concerns through their ongoing program groups, regular meetings (including congregational service), and other channels of communication.

The evangelism program supports other programs in tasks that provide opportunites for personal evangelism through witnessing, personal ministry, and mission projects. It works through the Church Council to focus and maximize all the evangelistic efforts of the church through development of a comprehensive church strategy of evangelism.

Tasks of Evangelism

A church can look to its evangelism emphasis program to accomplish three tasks of major importance in achieving the church's mission.

1. Engage the church in evangelism by developing a comprehensive church strategy of evangelism.

2. Involve church members in personal evangelism.

3. Reach persons for Christ through special events and mass evangelism.

These are church tasks for which the church-elected leaders of the evangelism program are made responsible. Here is a summary of the important church work included in each of these tasks.

Tasks 1: Engage the Church in Evangelism by Developing a Comprehensive Church Strategy of Evangelism

A church that takes seriously the Lord's commission to witness and make disciples must have a strategy and process to evangelize the lost. The evangelism program leaders (evangelism council) will assist the pastor in leading the church to develop and implement a simple, aggressive, and ongoing church strategy for evangelism, based on evangelistic needs and available resources.

It is important to understand certain key words in this task. *"Developing"* is used to mean "establishing a climate for evangelism and working out a plan that will enable the church to fulfill its evangelistic responsiblities in its setting." It is a workable process to bring people to Christ. *"Comprehensive"* means "including every approach that will enable the church to reach its evangelistic opportunity." This will involve all other programs as appropriate for their tasks. *"Strategy"* means "a major course of action, usually including several action plans and commitment of resources, to achieve a predetermined purpose." More specifically, in this task it means the plan for reaching the lost, which evangelism program leaders will lead the church in developing.

The evangelism program leaders should work with the pastor to develop a statement of the church's evangelistic purpose, based on a sound biblical theology of evangelism. This statement should be communicated to the congregation. Evangelism program leaders will also help create an atmosphere for evangelism and lead in determining evangelistic needs.

Examples of activities that will be included in a comprehensive evangelism strategy for a church include prayer for spiritual awakening, renewal in the lives of members, discovering evangelistic prospects, praying for the lost by name, training personal witnesses, participating in evangelistic visitation, preparing for and conducting revivals, and following up new Christians. The strategy should make full use of the evangelism tasks and evangelism training potential of other church programs, as discussed earlier in this chapter; and all efforts should be coordinated into the total church strategy through the Church Council.

Evangelism program leaders will take the lead in seeing that adequate leadership, calendar time, and finances are provided for the strategy, according to church policy and in light of the specific assignments to be carried by each church program.[5]

Task 2: Involve Church Members in Personal Evangelism

This task means to enlist, equip, and engage persons in sharing the gospel of Christ with another person in order to bring the unsaved person to repentance and faith, to a commitment to Jesus as Lord and Savior, and into the fellowship of a local church where the believer will be able to become spiritually mature and will be a witness of the gospel to others. "We must believe the scriptural teaching that every person without Christ is lost and hell is their destiny. We must pray for a burden about them and for courage to witness to them."[6]

Fred White, associate vice-president for evangelism at the Home Mission Board believes that "equipping and multiplying are vital to the life of the church. Every believer witnesses for or against Jesus. This task places the responsibility for enlisting and equipping witnesses on church evangelism program leaders, particularly the personal evangelism director. These leaders are to study witness training processes of all programs and recommend which is best for the church at a given time. When any other program's training is involved, cooperative efforts will be necessary between programs.

Whatever witness training program is used, it should involve as many people as possible."[7]

Evangelism program leaders will work closely with other programs to emphasize and provide witness training, to enlist persons in witness training and involve them in witnessing, and to follow up new Christians to enroll them in church programs in order to help them to grow toward spiritual maturity. The new Christian encourager plan can be an effective means of incorporating new Christians into the life and work of the church.

Task 3: Reach Persons for Christ Through Special Events and Mass Evangelism

This task means to present the gospel of Jesus Christ in cooperation with other programs through special events such as media, recreation, resort evangelism, Scripture and literature distribution, and mass evangelism such as revivals, crusades, rallies, marketplace and institutional evangelism.

Southern Baptist churches have been effective in reaching people for Christ through revivals, crusades, and special events. Public proclamation of the gospel and a strong invitation have enabled us to reach hundreds of thousands of people annually.

With the variant life-styles being expressed today, more creative ways of attracting persons' attention and presenting the gospel to them are needed. Your church can study its community, discovery various groups who need Christ, and devise a strategy to take the gospel where they are. Help is available for all these tasks from your association, state convention, and the Home Mission Board's Evangelism and Missions Sections [Woman's Missionary Union, Brotherhood Commission, and Sunday School Board].

Evangelistic events conducted outside the church building may be the avenue for attracting people with different life-styles. Special evangelistic projects are often attractive to unbelievers and will often be the means of creating interest in spiritual things.

Intensive efforts must be made to evangelize target groups such as ethnics, language groups, deaf, poor, rich, and others who may need an extra effort if they are to be reached. Churches must take the gospel where people are instead of expecting them to come and hear it.[7]

Leaders and Organization for Evangelism

The recommended leaders for the evangelism emphasis program are an evangelism director, mass evangelism director, and personal evangelism director. In small churches and church-type missions, one person may perform the duties of all three of these leaders. Most churches will want to add representatives from basic programs (pastoral ministries, Bible teaching, Church Training, Music Ministry, Woman's Missionary Union, and Brotherhood) on a temporary or continuing basis. Larger churches may find the need to enlist and equip evangelism specialists to assist in specific projects such as evangelistic people search, revival preparation, and the like. When these leaders meet to plan, coordinate, and evaluate evangelism efforts of the church, they are called the evangelism council (replacing the evangelism committee that has been recommended in the past).

To be successful, the evangelism program needs strong pastoral leadership supported by the evangelism council and full involvement of other programs through the Church Council in developing and carrying out plans for evangelistic efforts. The evangelism director will be a regular member of the Church Council. The evangelism director, personal evangelism director, and mass evangelism director should be elected annually according to church plan, as leaders for other programs are. In order for the church to gain full benefit of the training and experience received by these leaders, a built-in rotation plan like that common for committees is not recommended.

Is reaching persons for Christ being given high priority throughout your church programs? Are the program tasks designed to involve God's people in evangelism being given the strong emphasis they should have in a church on bold mission?

✎ :::

Pause and Do: *Personal Learning Activity 15*
1. List all church tasks that relate directly to reaching people for Christ. Indicate which program is assigned the task. By each task in your list, indicate how

well you think your church is doing that task. Use the common grading system: A—extremely well; B—rather well; C—average; D—poorly, and F—failing. (Any task of a program your church does not have should receive an F unless your church is doing that work in some other way.)

2. Does your church currently have an Evangelism Council (or committee)? If not, who is responsible for the three evangelism program tasks?

3. List and describe two personal witnessing efforts that are currently in progress in your church or have been carried on in recent months.

4. What do your answers to questions 1-3 suggest to you about the priority of evangelism in your church?

::: 🖑

---

[1]Robert L. Hamblin, vice-president, Evangelism Section, Home Mission Board, SBC, from resource material prepared for this book.

[2]John R. Bisagno and Harry M. Piland, *'Til Millions Know* (Nashville: Convention Press, 1983), pp. 76-77.

[3]"SBC Inter-Agency Glossary" (Prepared by the Coordinating Committee, Inter-Agency Council, SBC), p. 3.

[4]Fred E. White, associate vice-president, Evangelism Section, Home Mission Board, SBC, from resource material prepared for this book.

[5]Ibid.

[6]Ibid.

[7]Ibid.

CHAPTER 10

Providing for Essential Church Concerns

This chapter describes four emphasis programs as defined in chapter 3: family ministry, stewardship, vocational guidance, and student ministry. The two other emphasis programs, mission development and evangelism were discussed in chapters 8 and 9.

An emphasis program can help a church keep an area of major concern in proper focus by identifying needs, suggesting approaches to meet those needs, and working cooperatively through the Church Council to involve other programs in projects and activities related to their tasks in the area of concern.

Family Ministry

"Family Ministry is a distinctly biblical ministry," said Douglas Anderson, director of the Family Ministry Department of the Baptist Sunday School Board. He continued:

> Our Christian faith is profoundly a faith rooted in relationships. Our faith begins not with a creed but with a personal experience with Jesus Christ. The good news of our witness is that we are called into a reconciled relationship with the Heavenly Father, a newfound relationship in which we experience acceptance, affirmation, forgiveness, and belonging. All these experiences with Jesus have a direct bearing on what it means to be a family.
>
> I believe that family ministry is at the heart of what it means to be church. God calls us into relationships, and church is that place where we can learn to be the family of God. Most of us do need help in learning how to live in relationships. Make no mistake about it, living in reconciled relationships is fundamental to the Christian faith.
>
> We first encounter Jesus as an infant, coming to us in the arms of a family. The good news of Jesus Christ begins to be told in the context of human relationships, His family. It is with deep purpose, I believe, that God revealed Himself through Jesus in the midst of family relationships. The family was created by God, and the family continues to be God's special creation. All this is to say that the mission and ministry of the Christian church must be rooted in the concept of family ministry.[1]

How is it with the families of God's people today? Are the families of your church insulated from the pressures that affect other families in our culture? In recent decades the Christian concept of family has come under new attack from life-styles that were condemned as immoral or strongly "looked down on" in past generations.

In 1985, divorce shot up to a decade high; and experts aren't sure why. About half of all marriages end in divorce.[2] One report estimated that six out of ten marriages of women in their thirties would end in divorce.[3]

Every day on television and cable, in motion pictures, in contemporary music, in videocassettes, and in newspapers and magazines, our families are exposed to the presentation of family and individual life-styles that conflict with Christian family values. Negative values concerning personal relationships, family life, deviant life-styles, the place of Christianity in life, personal morality, sex, alcohol, drugs, and money and its use are communicated through these media and through the lives of many popular stars. Of growing concern is the increasing number of unwed mothers, many of them teenagers, and the increase in reported rape, incest, and child abuse. Added pressures are placed on many families as a result of both parents working outside the home, divorce, blended families, and one-parent families. As our culture gives less and less support to Christian family values, God's people in the church must find increasingly effective ways to teach and support the quality of family life that God intended.

Persons Who Need Family Ministry

Family ministry in a church has but one task—to minister to the distinctive needs of couples, parents and their children, senior adults, and single adults. Its purpose is to help the church and its programs enrich family life—marriages, parenting, senior adulthood, and single adulthood—by meeting family-related needs of these groups.

Each of the groups mentioned has distinctive needs to which a church should give attention. *Couples* means "married husband and wife," but even cohabiting unmarried couples need the redemptive ministry of the church as it seeks to carry the message of Christ to them. *Parents and their children* covers a variety of family situations—married couples and their offspring living in the home, married couples and their grown children in and/or outside of the home; single parents and their children (including noncustodial parents); stepparents and adoptive parents and their children. Unmarried parents and their children should also be targets for redemptive ministry. *Senior adults* refers to persons in the retirement years, including those who have never been in the work force. *Single adults* includes all persons at least eighteen years of age who have never been married or who are divorced or widowed. Divorced and widowed persons are often referred to as *single again*.

Work of Family Ministry

If family ministry in a church is to be effective, church leaders will find it necessary to discover the needs of couples, of parents and their children, of senior adults, and of single adults. Based on up-to-date information about the needs of these groups, a church should provide enrichment, educational, and crisis intervention activities designed to meet these needs.

Family life education and crisis intervention are vital parts of a family ministry program. Needs related to living and growing are no less important than special needs at critical times. A preventive ministry must go hand in hand with a crisis ministry. Each church will need to set priorities in meeting the needs of these groups in order to avoid trying to do everything at once and not doing anything well. Family ministry will also be strengthened by training church members to minister. Such training can be offered through Church Training and other basic programs.

Responsibility for Family Ministry

Family ministry does not have a comprehensive program organization in a church. Churches are encouraged to have a family enrichment committee to assist church programs in providing for the needs of families and to provide family enrichment programs for couples, parents, and other family members. The committee may have from three to twelve members, depending on the size of the church. Some of the major duties recommended for this committee are: (1) develop and recommend to the Church Council a comprehensive plan for meeting the needs of families, (2) plan and conduct family life projects and programs through which family needs are properly met, (3) encourage and assist church programs in meeting the needs of families, and (4) coordinate plans and activities through the Church Council. (A complete list of duties for this committee and suggestions concerning its makeup and functioning are available in materials published by the Family Ministry Department, Baptist Sunday School Board.)

Some churches may also feel a need for a Single Adult Council or a Senior Adult Council to coordinate the church's efforts to meet the needs of these subgroups of adults. These councils are discussed in chapter 12.

Approaches for Family Ministry

Special projects or events such as study courses, workshops, seminars, retreats, periodical distribution, Christian Home Emphasis (from Mother's Day through Father's Day), and family life revivals are found to be effective family ministry approaches by many churches.

Other family enrichment education can be made available through Sunday School, Church Training, and church media library. Examples of Equipping Center modules that have been jointly developed by the Family Ministry and Church Training Departments of the Sunday School Board are *How to Lead Your Family in Bible Study and Worship; Home: Key to Christian Values;* and *Parent-Teen Relationships.*

Crisis intervention can be handled by the pastor, other church staff members, deacons (perhaps through deacon family ministry), laypersons, or referrals to professional counselors.

"Family ministry is not simply a matter of church committees or special family programs on marriage enrichment. A church must begin at the point of making ministry to families a primary objective of its mission, of its outreach program, and of its evangelistic thrust. Family ministry needs to be integrated into the total life of a congregation, rather than being another program among many. We call this method of doing family ministry an 'emphasis.' "[4]

✎ ::

Pause and Do: *Personal Learning Activity 16*

1. Who is responsible for family ministry in your church?

2. List and describe two family ministry events or projects that have been done in your church within the last year.

3. Describe two needs of families, singles, or senior adults to which you think your church should give special attention during the next twelve months.

::⌨

Stewardship

The stewardship emphasis program in a church should lead God's people to an understanding of and commitment to biblical concepts of individual and corporate stewardship. It is designed to accomplish two specific church tasks:

1. Develop Christian stewards.
2. Involve the church in supporting cooperative program ministries.

Stewardship Is Biblical[5]

Contrary to popular opinion, stewardship is more than a name to encompass modern church fund-raising activities. It has strong biblical foundations, beginning in creation. God's creative work reached its climax in the creation of people. We were made in the image of God (see Gen. 1:27) and were made stewards over the rest of creation (see Gen. 1:28).

The word *steward* shows the owner-manager relationship between God and persons in both the Old and New Testaments. The Greek word, *oikonomos*, means "a house manager or steward." As managers, persons are responsible for taking seriously that which God has entrusted to them. The responsibility of stewardship is a task begun in creation and magnified in redemption (see Col. 1:16-20). Christians are stewards in their Father's house (God's world).

Christ is Lord over all creation; creation finds its purpose in Christ; and only Christ gives meaning to the use of all things (see Col. 1:16-18). Many of Jesus' parables echo the theme of our accountability and our management responsibilities (Luke 12:13-21, 16:1-13). We are accountable to God as stewards and are to live in light of the lordship of Christ. Fulfillment of the church's mission to take the good news of God's love and redemption in Christ to all peoples of the world depends on the faithful stewardship of Christ's followers.

These fundamental biblical teachings—the ownership of God, the lordship of Christ, the accountability of man, and the mission of the church—are foundational to Christian stewardship. Christians are God's stewards—managers of life, influence, and resources.

Stewardship Is Personal

God created each of us as a unique person. He regards us individually, and each of us shall give an account of our personal stewardship and shall be judged accordingly (see 2 Cor. 5:10, 1 Cor. 4:2). For Christians who recognize their role as managers of God's material world, stewardship includes four responsibilities, all of which are considered in light of biblical principles.

We are responsible for how we earn our money.—We are to earn our money in ways consistent with biblical teachings. We should honor God in our choice of vocation and in our performance on the job. We should view a job as one expression of Christian commitment.

We are responsible for our spending.—Wasteful spending, spending for unworthy purposes, or misusing credit indicates that a Christian does not understand fully his role as a steward.

We are responsible for our giving (see 2 Cor 9:7).—Giving is a visible expression of stewardship. It is far-reaching because it impacts the support of church ministries. Giving money through our church will be determined by our understanding of God's giving to us (see 2 Cor. 8:9), our willingness to grow in giving (see 2 Cor. 8:7), and our commitment to Christ and His church (see 2 Cor. 8:1-5). The giving/serving attitude should identify a Christian's approach to life.

We are responsible for planning the final disposition of possessions.—A Christian's stewardship planning will include seeking to honor Christ through allowing Christian causes to receive a share of possessions that remain in an estate after death.

Stewardship Is Church-Centered

The Bible is clear that the church is both a developer of stewards and a steward. God has called His church—His people—to fulfill His mission, and this requires maturing and dedicated stewards. He has called us to disciple the nations. Southern Baptists have interpreted the Great Commission in terms of Bold Mission Thrust.

We are involved in leading churches to participate in Planned

Growth in Giving, a plan to call each Southern Baptist to make new commitments to growth and giving. A. R. Fagan, president of the Southern Baptist Stewardship Commission, believes: "Planned Growth in Giving affords Southern Baptists one of the greatest opportunities for spiritual growth in their history. Helping members grow and lifting the level of giving among Southern Baptists will strengthen individuals and improve our work in all areas." It also calls for greater financial support of associational and Cooperative Program ministries. Growth in giving is imperative and must be one of our priorities if we are to reach our potential and fulfill the dream and goal of Bold Mission Thrust.

Stewardship Requires Planning, Leadership, and Education
The pastor has a major role in developing stewards through preaching, teaching, and support. Church members who have been selected and elected by the church for leadership positions in all the church organizations have responsibility for developing Christian stewards.

A wise approach that can help a church develop stewards and involve members in the support of Cooperative Program ministries is to elect and organize a church stewardship committee. This committee should give attention to all stewardship-related matters including stewardship education and mission support concerns, budget matters, and procedures for handling funds that have been given through the church.

Stewardship education and mission support emphases can include stewardship Bible studies in Sunday School, study of Church Training materials such as the Equipping Center modules on financial planning or stewardship, money management conferences, the observance of Cooperative Program Day and Month, and the use of available stewardship development and Cooperative Program promotional materials and visual aids.

The stewardship committee should lead in developing, presenting, promoting, and committing the church budget. A worthy church budget should indicate the church's commitment to ministries in the association and those supported through the Cooperative Program. Methods for receiving, recording, disbursing, reporting, and auditing money given through the church should be carefully considered.

Sections may be added to the committee during a special emphasis such as a building campaign. The program, Together We Build, provides churches a proved way to practice good stewardship of the church's financial resources.

The committee also can serve the church by incorporating new approaches and information about needs into ongoing stewardship development and mission support activities and by using all available channels in the church, especially the basic programs. to develop stewards. The work of the committee calls for the development of an annual calendar of stewardship activities. While stewardship is biblical and personal, it "comes together" in a church setting.

The future is bright for Southern Baptists and stewardship. Ernest D. Standerfer and James L. Powell of the Stewardship Commission have said: "We applaud the pastors and churches who have sought to develop Christian stewards and involve members in mission support concerns. The challenge facing us is to recognize and respond to the great need among church members for growth in all areas related to stewardship. If that growth is realized, it will bring changes in life-styles and giving patterns. It could enable the church better to fulfill its mission and bring a new dimension of joy to those involved."

✎ ::

Pause and Do: *Personal Learning Activity 17*
1. Define Christian stewardship in your own words.
2. What are four responsibilities of a Christian steward?
3. What are the tasks of the stewardship emphasis program and what organization is suggested for it?

:::⊟

Vocational Guidance

Baptists have always sought to emphasize the worth of persons and to minister to the unique needs of each person in the name of

Christ. This belief in the worth and uniqueness of each person has led Southern Baptists to realize that an individual's choice of occupation is of major significance to the church.

Coupled with this is the doctrine of Christian discipleship, which defines all of the Christian's life in terms of his or her Christian calling. Each Christian should thus approach daily work as a part of the Christian calling. Based on these two doctrines, a church is led to give careful, well-planned vocational guidance to its members.

A church's vocational guidance emphasis program performs one task for a church: Educate in Christian vocation and guide persons in church occupation and adjustment.

The meanings of key words in this task are important. *Vocation* is the call of God to each follower of Christ to a life of discipleship and believer's ministry. *Occupation* is an activity in which one engages for the purpose of earning a livelihood. *Guidance* means "a process which enables a person to become more self-directing under God's leadership." *Vocational guidance* means "helping a person make decisions concerning the call of God to a life of discipleship and believer's ministry." *Church occupation* is used to mean "an occupation (place of ministry) requiring a God-called and gifted person who is supported or commissioned by a church or denomination."

A vocational guidance emphasis program is needed to assist the church in helping persons discover and have a clear understanding of their interests, aptitudes, gifts, and abilities in relationship to God and other people. Each person has a need to become more self-directing on the basis of personal understandings that are reliable, realistic, and authentically Christian. In the community of the church, counseling and guidance can be offered to lead persons to know themselves, to consider their choices in the context of Christian discipleship, and to mature in their occupational choices. Education in the Christian meaning of vocation, work, and occupational choice is foundational for the Christian.

In addition to this, the church must take major responsibility for helping persons understand the nature of God's call to church occupations and for developing their sensitivity to His call. There is also a need for confronting persons with opportunities to consider church occupations and to make decisions concerning God's call, and for nurturing those who are contemplating or have chosen a church occupation. The work of the Holy Spirit is unique in a person's understanding of God's leadership in occupational choice, in daily work, and in making career transitions.

As an emphasis program, vocational guidance does not have its own organization in a church. It may have church-elected leaders, or pastoral ministries leaders may serve in that capacity. All program leaders have responsibility for determining how vocational guidance can best be channeled through their organization.

Vocational guidance takes place during the regular meetings and activities of Sunday School, Church Training, WMU, Brotherhood, and Music Ministry. Congregational worship services provide important times for this emphasis and for presenting opportunities to make decisions. Commitment counseling should be done at the time of decision and following. Vocational guidance is also made available through counseling by pastor, staff, and others; conferences; retreats; and informational features at various times during the week.

Other vocational guidance approaches a church may find useful include observing Life Commitment Month; training church program leaders in vocational guidance methods; planning a career fair; establishing a careers corner in the church media library or another location; sponsoring parent conferences; and involving youth in special projects, such as Youth Week or missions projects in which they gain some experience in church occupations and other needed ministries.

Vocational guidance finds expression in at least six ways in a church.

1. Creating a climate in which youth and adults can freely explore God's leadership in choosing an occupation.

2. Providing systematic studies through the curriculum of Sunday School and Church Training.

3. Providing special projects (workshops, retreats, seminary, discussion groups, and worship services) emphasizing the content of vocational guidance.

4. Providing information about calling, occupations, and occupational choices.

5. Providing opportunities for persons to gain experience and training in church occupations.

6. Proper counseling and nurturing of persons who have made decisions for church occupations.

Vocational guidance in churches takes on added significance because of its relationship to Bold Mission Thrust. As Southern Baptists progress in their efforts to win persons to Christ, start new Sunday Schools and churches, and send more home and foreign missionaries to share the gospel, there will be a significant increase in the number of God-called persons needed to fill missionary, denominational, and church places of ministry. They will come from churches that have prayed, taught, preached, counseled, and nurtured persons to help them hear and respond in loving obedience to God's call to occupational or bivocational ministry. Many of these may be bivocational.

✎ ::

Pause and Do: *Personal Learning Activity 18*
    1. List any sermons, activities, or events in your church during the last year that provided some type of vocational guidance for your church members or challenged them to consider whether God may be calling them to a church occupation.
    2. List two ways your church could offer some type of vocational guidance to the members.

::⊜

Student Ministry

Since *A Church on Mission* was published in 1980, student ministry has been identified as a sixth emphasis program in a church. In January 1986, a workgroup of the Coordinating Committee of the Southern Baptist Inter-Agency Council completed over two years of work on an updated design for student ministry on campuses and in Southern Baptist churches. The workgroup was led by Charles H. Johnson, director of the National Student Ministries Department of the Sunday School Board, and included representatives of all Southern Baptist Convention agencies, institutions, and commissions that relate significantly to students—Woman's Missionary Union, state convention directors of student ministry, campus program directors, and Baptist colleges. Out of that workgroup's study came a new recognition of the fact that churches need help in ministering to the needs of students and others in the academic community who are within their reach.

The need for student ministry is not limited to churches in towns or cities in which a college or university is located. Many, if not most, Southern Baptist churches have within their membership or among their prospects students enrolled in higher education who have special needs for loving ministry because of their life situation. The increasing number of students who commute daily, weekly, or frequently from home to college increases the need for churches that may not be in college communities to make adequate provision for ministry to students.

The Purpose of Student Ministry

The purpose of student ministry is to assist in fulfilling the mission of the church by leading students and others in the academic community to faith in God through Jesus Christ as Savior and Lord, to guide them in Christian growth and discipleship, and to involve them in responsible church membership.

The Nature of Student Ministry

On a college or university campus, student ministry functions as a basic program on behalf of the churches. It implements its tasks directly with students and others in the academic community by providing program activities and organizational structure as needed, with Baptist Student Union being its basic organization.

In a church, however, student ministry functions as an emphasis program and accomplishes its tasks primarily through other church programs, especially the basic programs. Any additional program activities or organizational structures are provided only to meet needs that are not or cannot be met through existing programs.

The Tasks of Student Ministry

In designing the student ministry program, the workgroup concluded that student ministry tasks should be the same on campus and in the churches but that they would be carried out in different ways, as indicated in the previous paragraph. This means that the tasks which are needed for campus student ministry, where the program has primary responsibility for implementing them, are similar to tasks of basic programs in a church, where basic programs have primary responsibility for ministering to students; and student ministry is an emphasis program. It also means that student ministry has more tasks than any other church program because its tasks must provide for all major work that a campus program needs to do. All who are interested in ministering to students in the churches should keep this important distinction in mind when planning to meet student needs.

Here is a brief overview of the nine student ministry tasks.

Task 1: Witness to persons about Christ.—The campus is one of the greatest mission fields in our world. Christian witness involves the verbal witness and all aspects of life which communicate the good news about Christ to unsaved persons and bring them to confess Jesus as Lord and accept Him as Savior. It includes sharing the good news with persons in normal, daily contacts. All Christians involved in student ministry are to be witnesses.

To accomplish this task student ministry leaders need to identify and locate lost students, train students to evangelize the lost, and involve and support students in witnessing. Any time a church is making a special witnessing effort, it should give special attention to involving students in reaching fellow-students and others in the academic community.

Task 2: Lead students into responsible church membership.—Responsible church membership by students is achieved by joining a local church and by participating in the programs of that church and in denominational activities. Students need the church for the relationships, guidance, support, and opportunities for service it provides. Likewise, the church needs the service and commitment to Christ the student brings into that fellowship. Students need to be challenged to become a part of God's work and to be shown how their gifts and abilities can be used in Christian service through a local church and the denomination. Church members and student ministry leaders will help students see the importance of being involved in a local church and in denominational life.

Task 3: Develop ministries to persons.—All persons have needs, but the academic community contains significant subgroups such as internationals, ethnics, and students away from home for the first time, who have special needs. Some of these needs are more acute at certain times, such as when new students arrive on campus, holidays, and the end of a term.

This task involves identifying persons with special needs on campus and in the community, motivating and training persons to meet the needs, and providing opportunities and resources for ministry to others.

Task 4: Guide students in making life decisions.—Many of the following significant life decisions are made by college students—religious faith, personal life-style, occupational choice, singleness or marriage, whom and when to marry, and the size of family now or later.

This task makes student ministry leaders responsible for helping students identify God's leadership in their lives and leading them to make life decisions in the context of biblical concepts about calling, vocation, gifts, discipleship, and stewardship of life. It also includes helping students develop skills in seeking God's guidance and in decision making.

A church can provide personal counseling, group guidance, and support groups and use mass communication in regular meetings and special events to address the concerns of life decisions.

Task 5: Involve students in study of the Bible and Christian faith.—Students need a comprehensive firsthand study of the Bible and related areas in order to move toward maturity in their own relationship to Christ and to teach others also. Special effort should be made to help them apply in life situations what they learn so that study will lead to development of a life-style that reflects a commitment to the lordship of Christ. Such study should also help students examine academic disciplines from a Christian perspective.

This task can be accomplished by encouraging students to participate regularly in Sunday School, Church Training, and other study opportunities in the church and by providing effective teachers and leaders who know how to interest students and speak to their needs. Study groups can be provided on campus, and materials and encouragement for individual study can be offered.

Task 6: Involve students in missions.—This task includes teaching students about missions, engaging them in missions efforts, praying for missions, and giving to missions. The Baptist Young Women's and Baptist Young Men's organizations can provide these experiences for students in a church and, in some instances, on campus. Missions projects led by the Missions Development Council can provide other opportunities to involve students in direct missions. Participation by students in mission emphasis weeks, seminary missions conferences, national missions conferences, and weeks of prayer and special offerings for missions can also help them become meaningfully involved in missions and in hearing God's call to missions service.

Task 7: Lead students to worship.—Students need to be taught what worship is and how essential it is for their Christian growth. This task makes leaders of students responsible for providing worship opportunities for them, opportunities for them to lead in worship, and materials to assist them in worship. Leaders will encourage students to participate in personal, family, and corporate worship experiences.

Task 8: Build Christian fellowship.—Fellowship provides the opportunity to establish, maintain, and enrich personal relationships with Christ, with others, and with oneself. It also means a community of persons related through a common life and created in Jesus Christ by the power of the Holy Spirit. (See earlier discussion of *koinonia*, p. 12.)

Students need persons with whom to identify who care about them and share their lives. Involvement with their peers and others in church groups can meet this need. Special attention should be given to involving internationals, ethnics, married students, commuters, and other specialized groups in Christian fellowship.

In carrying out this task, student ministry leaders in a church need to develop the fellowship-building skills of leaders and students and to provide opportunities for building Christian fellowship, such as involving students in various ministry actions that strengthen fellowship and offer a variety of social and recreational activities.

Task 9: Involve students in world issues and social action.— *"World issues"* are those subjects, topics, or problems, such as war and peace, economics, race, poverty, and citizenship, which affect our world and need to be dealt with from the Christian perspective. *"Social action"* is the way we as Christians deal with the world issues and attempt to apply the Christian faith in a constructive, redemptive way.

To implement this task, student ministry leaders and students will need to (1) determine world issues and social action for study and involvement, (2) study world issues and social action, and (3) provide opportunities for involvement in redemptive social action that is consistent with Christian discipleship.

Organizaton for Student Ministry

Necessary organization for student mininstry in a church is provided primarily through organizational units of the basic church programs—pastoral ministries, Bible teaching, Church Training, Music Ministry, Woman's Missionary Union, and Brotherhood.

In the simplest organization for churches with few students, the pastor and the teacher of the Sunday School class that includes college students are the primary leaders of the student ministry program. Other leaders are added as units involving students are added.

As soon as the number of prospects, enrollment, available leaders, and facilities will permit, a church should organize one or more separate classes or groups exclusively for college students. Manuals for the basic church programs give guidelines for beginning and adding these units.

As the student ministry program grows, organization to achieve program coordination and to plan churchwide events should be added. But simplicity of organization should be a continuing goal. The Church Council should be the primary vehicle for formal coordination.

The Student Ministry Guidebook, published by National Student Ministries Department of the Sunday School Board, explains how to progress from the simplest organization to a greatly expanded one in which a staff member may be responsible for student ministry and a Student Ministry Council is structured, consisting of representative leaders and members of the basic program organizations.

However student ministry is organized, responsibility should be clearly placed for such activities as conducting special studies, distributing *The Student* magazine, and planning and conducting special emphases such as Join the Church Day, Student Day at Christmas, and Student Awareness Month. Also, there should be a clear understanding about who will represent student ministry concerns on the Church Council.

For Bold Mission Thrust to succeed as it should, churches need to give more attention to college and university students. Christian students need to be enlisted in outreach, witness, ministry, and missions projects through which the gospel can be proclaimed. Unsaved students need to hear the gospel from their peers or from other church members. Out of the college student group will come most of our church, denominational, community, state, and national leaders of the future. Bold Mission Thrust requires that we win as many of them as possible to the Lord and to a Christian lifestyle and that we lead and equip Christian college students to be bold witnesses.

Pause and Do: *Personal Learning Activity 19*

1. Approximately how many college students are members of your church or its organizations? (If you don't know, ask someone in your church who might know.)

2. Which leader or staff member in your church is considered responsible for student ministry?

3. List any special project, study, or event (such as Student Day at Christmas or Student Awareness Month) that has involved college students in your church within the last year.

[1]Douglas Anderson, director, Family Ministry Department, Baptist Sunday School Board, from resource material prepared for this book.

[2]Paul Clancy, "Divorce hits puzzling decade high," *USA Today,* 24 Mar. 1986, p. 1A.

[3]Paul Claney, "For women in 30's, 6 of 10 marriages fail," *USA Today,* 4 Apr. 1986, p. 1A.

[4]Anderson.

[5]The section on stewardship is adapted from resource material prepared for this book by Ernest D. Standerfer, Stewardship Commission, SBC. Quotations are also drawn from that material.

CHAPTER 11

Helping a Church Function Effectively

God's people today live in a world in which knowledge and technology are expanding at a breathtaking rate. Numerous observers refer to our age as the Information Age. Advances in computer technology, satellites and other electronic communication, word processing, and photocopying have given us the capacity to acquire, use, store, and retrieve vast amounts of information in new ways. Our society is becoming increasingly complex and specialized. Persons in places of leadership and decision making find it necessary more frequently to call on specialists in technical fields to provide consultation, information, or other resources that will help them plan, develop new ideas, or make decisions.

Churches have felt a similar need and doubtless will feel it even more as we move toward the twenty-first century. Out of that need, Southern Baptists have identified three church programs that exist to be supportive to the entire church and the other programs in fulfilling the church's mission. We classify them as service programs. They are media library, recreation services, and administrative services.

Media Library

The media library program is designed to unify a church's efforts to involve media in the life of its members and the work of its programs. Church members, their families, and church prospects are increasingly accustomed to seeing effective use of print and audiovisual media at home, in school, and in community activities. This fact intensifies the need for a church to use the most up-to-date and effective media available for communicating God's Word and for teaching and training God's people to be on bold mission. Churches will find no better way to assure the availability of informational media than through an organized media library program.

Media Library Tasks

The media library program performs three service tasks for a church. Let's review them to determine what each includes.

Task 1: Provide media and media library services.—The word *media* in this task and in the name of this program means any device for use in transmitting information from an originator to a recipient. Media are teaching and learning tools which supply and communicate information. The two general types of media are printed and audiovisual.

A *media library service* is a group of actions taken by media library personnel to facilitate the use of media in special ministries, in personal study, in teaching and training, and in reaching people. Availability of media is the key. The media library exists in a church to assure the availability to these tools.

The media provided include those which are selected by the media library staff for general use and those which are suggested by leaders and members. The media library is more than a collection of books. Some of the types of media included are (1) printed materials of all types, (2) projected visuals and audiovisuals, (3) audio materials, (4) audiovisual equipment, (5) nonprojected visuals, (6) other miscellaneous materials, and (7) music resources.

Media library services may involve the use of selected media, the media library facilities, and/or the use of the media library staff. Examples of such services are audiovisual preview sessions; BTN administration; Bold Mission Thrust information center; career corner; audio and videocassette taping and duplication services; guided study programs; *Home Life* distribution plan; ordering, storing, and distributing tracts; story and film hours; study course records; and ordering, storing, and distributing church literature.

Media are provided by lending, giving, and/or selling through the church's media library. The media library should be open before and after all major meetings of the church and the church programs. Some media libraries are open during the meeting times of educational programs. Others are open for periods during the week. It is desirable for the media library location to be easily accessible to the people as they move from one church activity to another. Media can also be provided wherever needed—mission points, weekday classes, retreats, and "branch libraries" in large educational facilities.

The media library staff (1) select media needed for individuals and church programs, (2) secure media for stores and agencies, (3) record BTN messages for use when needed, (4) process, catalog, and store media, and (5) circulate media by lending, selling, or giving.

In providing services, staff members work with church leaders and members to identify their needs and follow church budgeting and spending procedures to secure necessary approvals, space, money, and personnel. They work with program leaders in establishing systems and understandings regarding the use of media and in maintaining and improving the services offered.

Task 2: Promote the use of media and media library services.— Promotional activities are needed to make church members, leaders, and prospects aware of available media and to encourage them to use those which relate to their life and work.

The media library staff try to determine the needs of the various target groups by studying information about dated curriculum, special events, seasonal interests, and the personal concerns of individuals. They use this information to plan promotional activities suitable to reach each target group.

Examples of promotional activities are audiovisual previews, bookmarks, book talks, brochures, bulletin boards, bulletin inserts, church bulletins and papers, letters and cards, media fairs, media library emphasis week, posters and signs, displays, and skits.

Task 3: Train persons in media skills.—Church leaders and members often need guidance and help in understanding the value of media in their personal lives and church activities. They need training in how to select appropriate media and equipment and how to use them effectively in learning, teaching, ministering, and witnessing.

The media library staff discover which media skills are needed by observing the use (or nonuse) of media, consulting with program leaders about needs of their workers and by doing surveys of members and leaders. Using this information as a guide to planning, they work with program leaders and church staff to provide needed training activities. Examples of training approaches are periodical orientation sessions for all church leaders, individual conferences, special workshops, presentations in regular meetings, circulation of media about media, and guidance in the use of BTN messages.

The Bold Mission Thrust information center is one way the media library can support a church's outreach efforts. A crucial and continuing need is for church leaders and members to have the latest information about opportunities, resources, and needs related to Bold Mission Thrust. The media library can meet this need by securing materials from the association, state convention, and Southern Baptist Convention agencies and by displaying them in the Bold Mission Thrust information center.

Mancil Ezell, director of the Sunday School Board's Church Media Library Department characterizes media library's service in these words: "As the Bold Mission Thrust emphasis reaches its peak of impact, the church media library continues to serve as the information center. When church persons and organizations use enrichment and learning resources, the media library is performing its mission and ministry. Information channels such as print media, visual media, and telecommunication assist churches in touching, reaching, teaching, growing, equipping, and discipling lives!"[1]

✎ ::

Pause and Do: *Personal Learning Activity 20*
Describe three ways a media library can help God's people be more effective in fulfilling their mission.

::⬚

Recreation Services

Recreation plays a positive role in helping a church be on bold mission. Sports, all types of recreational leisure activities, and physical fitness and exercise are high on the priority list of millions of people, as either participants or spectators. Because of these interests, some persons who may never repond to other approaches can be reached for Christ and the church through recreational activities.

Recreation is activity designed to develop, to restore, and to refresh the individual. It is both serious and purposeful and can assist persons toward fuller discovery of self.

The service role of recreation in a church is twofold. First, it can play a conductive role as the functions of a church find expression in the recreational activities themselves, as when a Christian drama is used to proclaim the gospel and call persons to decision. Second, by providing ideas, tools, and methodologies for use by other church programs, it supports the activities of other programs and the entire congregation. Christian discipleship includes stewardship of time including leisuretime, those blocks of unoccupied time in which a person is free to do what he chooses. Church recreation can help a faithful Christian steward use leisure in constructive and healthy ways.

The Task of Recreation Services

Recreation's task is to provide recreation methods, materials, services, and experiences that will enrich the lives of persons and support the total mission of the church.

Notice that this task sets recreation in the context of helping to fulfill the church's mission, which is its rightful place. Any recreational activities sponsored by a church should contribute in identifiable and worthy ways to the church's mission in the world.

The program of recreation services will achieve its purpose when it serves as a channel of service and support, a catalyst in outreach, a vehicle for ministry and mission action, a tool for teaching, an avenue for abundant living, an aid to worship, and an environment for fellowship.

A church which recognizes its responsibilities to the whole person—physical, social, mental, and spiritual—will find recreation helpful in meeting a variety of human needs. Recreation services has responsibility for providing a wide variety of recreational activities and materials that will enrich the lives of those involved and will support the total purpose of the church. The most common types of church recreation are briefly discussed in the next section.

Types of Recreation for a Church

The wide variety of recreational activities available for church use can appeal to many different interests and meet numerous needs in the lives of church members, their families, and prospects for the church.

Social recreation is leisuretime activity which involves social interaction—people with people—in an appropriate setting. It usually finds expression as a party, banquet, fellowship, picnic, or some similar activity. Social recreation enables people to have wholesome fun in a Christian setting. It provides opportunities for meeting new people, finding love and Christian witness, strengthening established relationships, and having experiences that aid social growth.

Social recreation helps build *koinonia*—the fellowship of believers in Christ—as people play, laugh, and sing together. Social recreation can help Christians realize anew they belong to God and to one another.

Social recreation can be an effective means of outreach to persons who need Christ and the church, especially those who will not respond initially to attempts to involve them in Bible study, worship, or other church activities.

Sports and games include any type of physical or mental game or contest where teams or individuals place their skills and abilities in opposition to those of others. The purpose of sports and games is competition and enjoyment, fellowship, and physical exercise of the body.

A Christ-centered and properly directed sports program can provide opportunities for individuals to give or receive a positive Christian witness, have joyous Christian fellowship, and develop desirable personal qualities such as honesty, self-control, responsibility, sportsmanship, and teamwork that contribute to building strong Christian character. It can encourage children, youth, and adults to identify themselves more boldly with the mission of the church.

Sports activities in the local church are usually categorized as *team sports,* such as soccer, flag football, softball, baseball, basketball, and volleyball; *lifetime sports,* such as archery, bicycling, boating or sailing, golf, and hiking; *individual sports,* including the activities of hunting and fishing, gymnastics, skating, skiing, bowling, and horseback riding; and *dual sports,* such as tennis, badminton, horseshoes, table tennis, handball or racquetball, and croquet.

Christian drama can portray the Christian life and the conflict of forces relating to it. It can also help persons explore their relationship to God, to others, and themselves. Church drama should communicate Christian concepts rooted in biblical truth.

Experience has shown drama to be a powerful means of communication that will communicate to many persons who may be turned off by traditional sermons and church services. A church on bold mission may find it to be a major means for reaching such persons.

Church drama includes storytelling, clowning, puppetry, monologue, improvisation, creative dramatics, choral drama, mime/pantomime, tableau, music drama, play production, fun drama, readers theater, and multimedia.

Camping uses the resources of the natural environment for Christian education, fellowship, evangelism, ministry, and personal growth experiences. It uses the creation to teach about the Creator.

Types of church camping include retreat camping, travel camping, day camping, resident camping, wilderness camping, backpacking, primitive or pioneer camping, Christian stress camping, family camping, and adventure recreation.

Recreation music is vocal and/or instrumental music used by an individual or a group in a recreation or leisure setting for pure fun and enjoyment or for fellowship and worship. It can be an effective support to recreational activities such as banquets, parties, fellowships, and retreats by stimulating people to participate. Singing, playing simple musical instruments, and simply listening to a musical performance call for a degree of participation. In some instances recreation music may become the featured activity, as in an all-church fellowship which is primarily singing, musical games, or musical stunts.

A *retreat* is a time and place for church members to disengage from the daily routines and mundane affairs of life, not because they have no rightful demands upon us, but because we often let them consume too much of life. The principle of retreat is withdrawal. Its aim is to deepen one's knowledge of God, of His love and His design for life, and of oneself in relationship with God and other persons. It provides opportunity for solitude and introspection—time to think, pray, talk, and listen, and time for the Christian to look upward, inward, and outward (in that order). Out of confrontation with God in retreat can come a servant life that is integrated and ordered by a stronger covenant relationship with Christ.

Four broad categories of retreats are: church leadership, age-group, organizational, and special emphasis.

Arts, crafts, and hobbies are activities that involve an individual in the use of his hands to create, to form an expression of the culture of the moment or of his or her own personality. Such activities provide occasions for constructive use of leisure and for Christian fellowship among kindred spirits involved in a common endeavor. Their appeal may strengthen a church's outreach and ministry in the community.

Physical fitness means having good health—the ability to perform daily work effectively without undue fatigue, to survive unexpected physical emergencies, and to have sufficient energy remaining to enjoy the recreational pursuits of leisure. In the psychological sense, it relates to how one looks and feels—mentally, emotionally, and physically. Physical fitness does not come automatically but must be developed and maintained by a regular, ongoing program of conditioning and nutrition.

Physical fitness is becoming a high priority concern in our culture. Because care for the body is a concern of Christian stewardship of life, churches have an interest in encouraging God's people to take care of their bodies. Churches can do this by making guidance and program suggestions available. Some churches provide facilities and equipment for members to use in achieving and maintaining physical fitness.

Therapeutic recreation is the provision of leisure ministries to persons of special need, such as the blind, deaf, retarded, emotionally maladjusted, crippled, and otherwise handicapped. Therapeutic recreation may help these persons find satisfying recreational outlets that can continue throughout life. It may help them live a normal and useful life in society and, in some cases, help them recover health.

Responsibility for Church Recreation Services

Leaders enlisted and elected according to the church's plan carry responsibility for providing recreation methods, materials, services, and experiences. The recreation director, as a program leader, is a member of the Church Council. Suggestions for beginning with a simple organization and expanding it to meet growing church needs are given in administrative materials developed by the Church Recreation Department of the Baptist Sunday School Board.

✎ ::

Pause and Do: *Personal Learning Activity 21*
List at least three ways your church could use (or is using) recreation as a means of outreach, witnessing, and ministry.

::◁

Administrative Services

From a study of New Testament church life, "it is apparent that government of the local church of the New Testament was in the hands of all the people rather than in the hands of a small group of rulers. . . . The whole church bore the responsibility for church government. Although both pastor and deacons had special responsibilities, the assembly was the governing unit."[2]

Based on this pattern, a Baptist church is its own governing body under the lordship of Christ and alone is responsible for all necessary administrative work. But it is impractical, if not impossible, for the assembled congregation to handle all the details of administration. A church works more effectively when the congregation uses its business meeting time to set policies and make major decisions about the church's life and work. As preparation for these decisions, it can wisely delegate to officers and committees the responsiblity for doing the detailed and time-consuming work necessary to study, plan, and develop recommendations about administrative policies and procedures, solutions for administrative needs or problems in the church, and recommended plans of action for the church. In the context of Philippians 4, each congregation can seek out those members who have specialized administrative gifts, skills, and interests and call on them to serve the church in their area of specialty.

In so doing, the church provides them opportunity for fulfillment in service to the church.

Task of Administrative Services

The task of administrative services is to assist the church to plan its program, manage its resources, and govern its life and work.

A proper understanding of the key words in this task is important. *Assist* means to give support and aid. The work of administrative services is not to make decisions for the church but to help the church make necessary decisions. A church may have problems if the congregation gives up too much of its rightful authority for decision making to church staff, officers, and committees. To secure needed assistance, the church assigns necessary administrative work to groups or individuals and requires them to report to the church on their assignment.

Plan simply means determining a mode of operation and a course of action. *Manage* means to direct or carry on the business affairs of the church as requested or assigned to support the church in fulfilling its mission. A church may assign to an individual or committee responsibility for day-to-day operational activities in an administrative area within church policies and procedures.

Govern means to guide and direct. It refers to those means by which a church regulates or rules its affairs.

Responsibility for Administrative Services

In Southern Baptist churches, it is common practice to assign responsibility for administrative work to general church officers, church committees, church staff members, and the Church Council. Each church will decide which officers, committees, and staff members it needs in order to be on bold mission.

General church officers.—Church officers are elected by the church on recommendation of the nominating committee. It is suggested that they serve for three-year terms and be allowed to succeed themselves. They report to the church. The following officers are suggested for a church of any size.

• A moderator's principal function is to plan and conduct the church business meeting and to coordinate the work of church officers and committees. The pastor serves as moderator in many churches, but the moderator may be another church member elected to that office. In the absence of the moderator, the chairman of deacons or an elected church member may serve as moderator.

• Trustees act as the legal agents of the church. (In some churches the trustees may act as the property and space committee.) Three to nine persons chosen from the church generally serve three years, with one to three (one third) of the trustees' terms expiring each year.

• The church treasurer assists in the receiving, accounting, and disbursing of all the church's monies. Assistant(s) to the treasurer should be added as needed.

• The church clerk records and keeps in permanent form all official actions of the church and makes this information available on request.

Church administrative committees.—Church committees are elected by the church upon recommendation of the nominating committee. The term of office is usually three years with the terms of one third of the members expiring each year.

Committee officers include a chairperson, a secretary, and other officers as needed. A committee may have a vice-chairperson if needed.

Church committees report to the church. In some instances, especially in small churches or churches having few adults, one person may be elected to function in place of a committee.

Guidance materials developed by the Church Administration Department of the Sunday School Board in cooperation with other programs assist churches in identifying and structuring committees they need. The materials provide suggested principal function, membership, and specific duties for each committee. Here is an overview of the most common committees.

• The nominating committee leads in staffing all church-elected positions filled by volunteers, including vacancies occurring during the year. Three to twelve members, depending on church size, serve on this committee. They meet with the Church Council when necessary.

• The church property and space committee assists the church in the care of all property and buildings; studies and recommends the use of space and furnishings as they relate to church programs and activities; studies needs and recommends acquiring property and creating space that seems necessary; resolves property and space problems in the Church Council through its chairman; and administers work assigned to it. The committee's three to fifteen members, depending on the judgment of the church, should include representatives of church programs.

• The flower committee provides appropriate flowers and related decorations to enhance congregational worship services and other services held in the sanctuary. Three to six members, depending on church size, are elected at large.

• The food services committee assists the church in administering its food services effectively. Three to twelve members serve, depending on church size.

• The history committee (1) assists the church in making and keeping accurate, comprehensive records of its current life and work; (2) gathers and safeguards all historical records of the church; (3) helps the church understand and learn from its own history; and (4) helps church members know and appreciate their large heritage as Baptists. Three to twelve members are needed, depending on church size.

• The personnel committee assists the church in matters related to employed personnel administration. Three to nine members serve, depending on church size.

• The public relations committee communicates the messages of the church to church members and the community. Three to twelve members are elected, depending on church size.

• The church weekday education committee assists the church in establishing and administering church weekday education. Three to twelve members are needed, depending on church size.

• The ushers committee assists participants and leaders before, during, and after congregational services. As many ushers as needed are elected, depending on church worship service attendance.

• The audio services committee operates and ensures proper maintenance of the sound reinforcement system for congregational worship services. Three to six members are chosen, depending on the need. Some specialized knowledge and technical skills are required to operate a sound system. Membership of this committee does not follow the rotation system.

Chapter 12 has information about the preschool committee, and chapter 10 includes information about the stewardship and family enrichment committees.

Church Council.—The Church Council is a key administrative services group for planning and coordinating the work of a church. Its membership and duties are discussed in the next chapter.

Pause and Do: *Personal Learning Activity 22*

1. Who is responsible for making the decisions necessary to plan, manage, and govern the affairs of the church?

2. Why does a church need administrative services?

3. List the names of the administrative services committees your church has, including any not listed in this chapter.

[1]Mancil Ezell, director, Church Media Library Department, Baptist Sunday School Board, from resource material prepared for this book.

[2]W. A. Criswell, *The Doctrine of the Church* (Nashville: Convention Press, 1980), p. 67.

CHAPTER 12

Coordinating a Church's Work

In chapters 3-11 of this book, we have identified the basic, emphasis, and service programs that can help God's people in a church to be on bold mission. We have considered the contribution each program can make to the life and work of God's people through its assigned tasks.

Whatever your church size and the number of programs it has, consider for a moment what would happen if pastoral ministries leaders, and each of the leaders of the other programs in your church, had different ideas about the church's mission and its priorities for a given year or quarter, or if each program leader planned the work of that program without checking with any of the others. Of course, the result would likely be wasted effort and emotional energy, conflicts of all types—in schedule, among leaders, and in use of facilities and other resources—and a low level of accomplishment in fulfilling the church's mission. Such a church would probably be about as effective as an automobile on which the front wheels try to turn in opposite directions or the gears in the transmission won't mesh; the power is wasted or not transmitted.

A church that wants to be effective on bold mission must learn to harmonize all its program activities into one forward thrust for Christ. All the programs must work in harmony toward achieving the church's mission and its goals for a given period of time so that maximum contribution can be made by each program. Every program must be committed to the health and effectiveness of the total body, the church. This harmonizing of the activities of individuals or groups into one plan of work to achieve common goals is called coordination.

The importance of coordination is intensified in Southern Baptist churches because of our cherished principles of democracy in participation, leadership through servanthood, the priesthood of believers, and the role of the congregation in governing the affairs of the church. Coordination is a necessity because each of the programs is responsible to the church for carrying out its tasks and not to any one human "chief executive" who makes all the important decisions. The need for coordination is further intensified by the number and complexity of programs that are needed in an active church to reach out with the gospel through witness and ministry and to meet the needs of church members and their families.

Coordination is needed at every level and in all phases of a church's organization. Much of the coordination can and should occur voluntarily without formal procedures or structures. In other instances formal methods and structures are needed.

Southern Baptist churches through the years have seen a need to coordinate at three levels in the church: (1) churchwide coordination of all programs—Church Council, (2) coordination of work within each program in proper relationship to the total church program—program council, and (3) the coordination of age-group work across program lines—self-coordination, coordinating councils or committees, and age-division coordinators or directors. The larger the church becomes and the more numerous and varied its programs, the greater the need for formal coordinating structures with establish policies.

Coordinating the Total Church Program—Church Council

One of the most important planning and recommending groups in a church is the Church Council. It is the one planning and coordinating group which has representatives of all the church's programs and which can take the comprehensive, overall look at what the church needs to be and to do in order to be on bold mission in its situation.

The Church Council services as a forum for a church's leaders to guide planning, coordinating, conducting, and evaluating the total work of the church. It depends on the various church organizations to carry out the church's program according to their assigned tasks. As chairman of the Church Council, the pastor is able to lead in developing a unified program that gives major attention to priority needs.

Who Is on the Church Council?

Each church must make its own decision about who serves on the Church Council, but many churches have discovered through experience that these church leaders should serve on the Council.

Pastor.—As general leader and administrator of the church, he usually serves as chairman.

Church staff members.—Any staff members whose responsibility is related to the entire operation of one or more church programs should be a member of the Church Council, for example, a minister of education, a minister of music, a minister of youth.

Directors of church programs.—The church-elected director of any programs the church has—Sunday School, Church Training, Music Ministry, Woman's Missionary Union, Brotherhood, Evanelism, Missions Development, media library, recreation services.

Chairman of deacons.—Deacons work with the pastor and staff in providing pastoral ministries for the church and in performing any other specific duties assigned by the church.

Chairperson of key committees.—The family enrichment and the stewardship committees are the organization for the emphasis programs of family ministry and stewardship. They should be represented on the Church Council by their chairpersons. At times the Church Council may ask the chairperson of other key committees to participate, at least for a time, in connection with discussion or plans involving their work.

Chairpersons of age groups or other councils.—If a church has such councils as youth ministry council, senior adult council, single adult council, or student ministry, the chairperson (or related staff member) should serve on the Church Council to ensure that any plans developed for these age-groups or subgroups within an age group are properly harmonized with the plans of church programs.

How Are Church Council Members Chosen?

Church leaders become members of the Church Council as a result of election as program director or committee chairperson, by being called to be pastor or staff members, or by being chosen as chairperson of any age-group coordination council or committee the church may have. Their term of office is the same as for the position which makes them members of the Church Council.

What Officers and Meetings Are Needed?

The officers of a Church Council are a chairman and a secretary. The pastor usually serves as chairman because of his role as general leader of the church. The secretary is chosen from the group by Church Council members, or the church clerk or a church staff secretary may serve. The chairman is responsible to the church for leading the Church Council in the performance of its duties. The secretary is responsible to the Council, under the supervision of the chairman, for providing secretarial assistance required by the Church Council.

Church Councils that are doing the most effective work usually meet monthly. Occasionally, a called meeting may be needed to deal with matters requiring attention before the next regular meeting.

What the Church Council Can Do for a Church

The principal function of a Church Council is to assist the church in determining its course and to coordinate and evaluate its work. A functioning Church Council can provide these more specific types of assistance for a church:

1. Help the church understand its mission and define its priorities.

2. Coordinate studies of church and community needs.

3. Recommend to the church coordinated plans for church program projects and activities and coordinate the church's schedule of activities, special events, and use of facilities.

4. Evaluate progress and the priority use of church resources.

As a Church Council seeks to carry out these specific duties, most of its work falls into three areas—planning, coordinating, and evaluating the church's total program in order to help the church achieve a balanced and effective ministry.

Planning

What church has sufficient time, money, and personnel to do everything that needs to be done in the community it serves? A church must set priorities and develop plans to make maximum use of available resources. A Church Council can help a church decide which ministries to provide immediately, which to schedule later, and which not to do at all. In determining priorities to recommend to the church, the Church Council should study carefully the nature and mission of the church, do in-depth study of the needs of persons in the surrounding community and of church members and their families, and seek the Holy Spirit's guidance through earnest prayer.

After priorities have been set in the planning process, work begins on developing church goals in the priority areas. A goal should state specifically what the church wants to accomplish—for whom, when, and where—in the priority area. For each goal, one or more specific action plans will be needed. An action plan outlines what specific work will be needed, in what sequence, by what date, and who will be responsible for each action. Action plans are usually assigned for implementation to church programs in relation to each program's tasks. For major efforts, some churches find it helpful first to decide on strategies which consist of several goals and action plans. (See the definition of *strategy* in chapter 9.) This kind of planning was referred to in chapter 3 as the statement of *dated intentions.*

For example, a church goal recommended by the Church Council in the priority area of witnessing to all lost and unchurched persons in the community might be "to witness to all the lost and unchurched persons within a three-mile radius of the church [by a set date]." This effort would be part of the church's comprehensive strategy for evangelism developed through the leadership of the evangelism program. The main thrust of the effort could be through the Sunday School, with other programs in supporting roles. One action plan could be a People Search and Scripture distribution project, similar to those in preparation for the 1986 Good News America revivals.

Coordinating

At the heart of the Church Council's work is the job of coordinating all the different program activities so that they fit together and work smoothly in correct relationship to one another like the parts of a fine watch. When the Church Council is doing its work, a church does not have to waste time and energy dealing with problems caused by programs scheduling activities that conflict in meeting time or use of facilities. Likewise, there is never any good reason for programs to offer similar activities that ought to be related to each other but aren't. For example, in a church without a Church Council, Sunday School, WMU, Missions Development, and evangelism might each schedule some type of community survey to identify persons to be reached, in keeping with their tasks. Such uncoordinated effort would be a waste of resources and could cause problems within the church and give people in the community a negative impression of the church.

Such problems can be avoided easily when Church Council members work together on developing a church calendar of activities on which all major church events are scheduled a year ahead of time.

In developing the calendar of activities Church Council members can schedule needed activities to achieve maximum effect for the total church program, the needs of church members and their families, and the needs of the church programs.

Coordination is simply teamwork. A good Church Council becomes a team that helps a church coordinate all of its activities into an effective total program. Such a coordinated program can make maximum use of all the resources the Lord entrusts to His people for carrying out His will.

Evaluating

The Church Council's role in evaluating is to help the church check up on how well it is doing and to learn from experience. After the completion of each major phase of a church's program, the Church Council should spend some time analyzing how it went and determining how the activity might be improved in the future. A church that does not evaluate its efforts and learn from them is likely to repeat the same mistakes. The Church Council helps prevent this by making concise evaluative reports to the congregation concerning the results of major church efforts.

The evaluation process includes several logical actions for the Church Council to take: (1) Set performance standards (expectations of achievement) as a basis for future evaluation. (2) Obtain accurate information about the work as it is being done and at completion of projects or action plans, (3) Compare the actual achievement with the standards that were set in advance. (4) Report the evaluation to the congregation with recommendations for improvement or change.

A Church Council should resist the temptation to spend so much time on planning and coordinating that little attention is given to evaluating. Good evaluating may save time in future planning and coordinating, and it is essential if a church is to learn well from experience.

Coordinating a Program's Work—Program Council

Each church program that has several officers and organizational units needs a program council to assist the program in determining its course, coordinating efforts of groups within the program, and relating to the Church Council for coordinating program activities with those of the whole church. The larger and more complex the organization of the program, the greater the need for a program council. The basic educational programs, Missions Development, and evangelism all recommend program councils. Media library and recreation services have councils in larger organizations.

A program council includes general officers and the directors of major units in the program. A person becomes a member of a program council when elected by the church to a program leadership position included on the council. The term of office corresponds to that of the church-elected program leadership position. It is common practice to elect leaders for one year and to let them succeed themselves.

A program council has these duties:

1. Help the program understand its mission and define its priorities in the light of church priorities.

2. Conduct studies of church and community needs related to program tasks.

3. Coordinate program activities and schedules.

4. Evaluate progress, effectiveness, and the priority use of church resources.

5. Report regularly to the church.

Coordinating Age-Group Work

Coordination of age-group work may be accomplished through self-coordination, coordinating councils or committees, or age division coordinators/directors. A church determines which approach to use in light of the size and complexity of organization within the age division.

Self-coordination exists when organization leaders within an age division voluntarily coordinate their work and the use of space, equipment, and supplies. It is the simplest approach, particularly well suited for small churches and age divisions with few workers.

A *coordinating council* may be established for an entire age division. It consists of leaders of departments, choirs, and other organizational units of a particular age division. Its principal function is to serve as a counseling, advisory, and coordinating group when self-coordination is not adequate. The chairperson may be one of the members of the council, elected by the members.

An example of such a council is the youth ministry council. Consisting of adult leaders of youth program organizations and three representative youth, its principal function is to coordinate the work of youth program organization units into a balanced, comprehensive ministry to youth. Each council member's term of office corresponds to that of his or her church-elected program leadership position. The chairperson is usually the person filling the role of youth ministry coordinator.

Some churches, especially larger ones, establish a preschool committee to coordinate work in that age division. Its principal function is to coordinate all activities and ministries of the various church organizations as they relate to preschool children. The committee is usually composed of three to twelve members elected according to church policy, depending on church size. It is recommended that the committee have a representative of each basic program, a father, a mother, and directors of Cradle Roll, day-care, and weekday programs.

Some churches, especially larger ones, find it helpful to establish a council to coordinate activities for a subgroup within an age division in order to meet special needs. Examples of these are senior adult council, single adult council, and student ministry council.

Each of these councils includes representatives of all church program units that include the group. Each council is represented on the Church Council by the chairperson for the group or by a related staff member.

The principal function of a senior adult council is to assist the church programs to become aware of and meet the needs of senior adults and to coordinate and promote weekday programs for senior adults.

A single adult council assists the church programs to become aware of and meet single adult needs. It plans and promotes enrichment programs for never married, divorced, and widowed persons. More detailed information about senior and single adult councils is available from the Family Ministry Department of the Sunday

School Board. (The student ministry council was discussed in chapter 10.)

Age-division coordinator or director is another approach to coordination. This position is usually elected by the church and is responsible to the pastor or minister of education. The principal function is to counsel age division leaders and coordinate the work of units within the age division, as assigned. Additional information about this position is available in materials produced by the Church Administration Department of the Sunday School Board.

Each church should design its own approach for coordinating its work. Structure and process for coordination should be kept as simple as possible. Coordination of effort must not be neglected in a church that wants to be effective on bold mission.

✎ ::

Pause and Do: *Personal Learning Activity 23*
  1. State the principal function of a Church Council.
  2. List and define briefly the three major types of work that a Church Council does for a church.
  3. If your church has a Church Council, what leaders serve on it? Compare your list with the list in this chapter. If not, how is the work of a council being done in your church?

:::⊜

Conclusion: Being God's People: a Southern Baptist Church on Bold Mission?

Notice that the title of this concluding section is the title of this book, but with a question mark added. Each fellowship of God's people called a Southern Baptist church has to determine for itself whether it is to be on bold mission with Him after the lost. Each church will determine whether this title applies to its life and work with a question mark or with an exclamation point.

If each resident member of every cooperating Southern Baptist church had won one person to the Lord in the 1984-85 church year, churches could have reported 10,298,106 baptisms. Instead, they reported baptizing 351,071, including children from church families. That is an average of one baptism for each 29.3 resident members, one for each 41.3 total members. Baptist Press quoted William Tanner, then president of the Home Mission Board, as saying that this is the third lowest number of baptisms in the last thirty-five years! He went on to express alarm that 6,669 Southern Baptist churches out of 36,979 did not report any baptisms in the 1984-85 church year.[1] And this is in spite of the fact that we are several years into our Bold Mission Thrust effort!

In 1954, J. N. Barnette, leader of Southern Baptist Sunday School work at that time, wrote a book entitled *One to Eight*. In it he challenged Southern Baptists to lower the ratio of baptisms to church members to one to eight. At that time, the ratio was about one baptism for every twenty church members, when we had about eight million church members (as compared with 14,486,403 in 1984-85).[2]

Is it too much to expect a church member to average winning one person to the Lord every twelve months if sharing the gospel is a top priority in his or her life?

Let's think about your church and mine. Consider its investment of time, leadership, and money in relation to the mission our Lord has given us. What does my church do best? In what types of activities do our most involved members spend the bulk of their time—worship, education, ministry to the needs of persons, witnessing, fellowship? Is our visiting directed more toward our church families and other Christians who might transfer their membership? Where do we spend more of our "church work" time—in activities with Christians at the church building or out among the lost and needy, sharing the love of Christ and our love with them? Are we so comfortable in the security and fellowship of activities at the church building that we don't have much time to visit the lost and unchurched or perform a ministry of love in the name of Christ to some person or group who is hurting?

What we do at the church building is extremely important. It is activity that motivates, challenges, teaches, equips, nurtures, proclaims the gospel, and builds fellowship. But most of it involves Christians and their families. Many churches have few lost persons (other than those in church families) coming to Bible study or worship. Visiting and ministering to church families is biblical and vital to a strong fellowship. Visiting Christian prospects for the church is worthy and needful.

But an essential and crucial part of the work of God's people needs to happen away from the church building—out in daily life where we model the gospel in life-style, share it by our words, and demonstrate it in our ministries of love and generosity toward persons of all types and cultures. Those persons have needs as varied as the colors of a rainbow, but their basic spiritual need is to experience God's love in a redemptive relationship with Him through Christ. Here is the mission of God's people. Here is Bold Mission Thrust, to be out among the lost and needy between our trips to the church building and to bring them to the church to hear more gospel if they will come.

Perhaps you have heard the question, What kind of church

would my church be if all the members were just like me? An old cliché, you say? Please don't dismiss it on that basis without considering it as a serious, probing question. How soon will every lost person in the world hear the gospel if all of God's people are just like you and me in their commitment and priorities? If all Southern Baptist churches are just like yours and mine in their commitment to evangelism and missions, what are the prospects that Bold Mission Thrust will gain momentum and become a mighty movement that captures hearts and mobilizes lives? What is the likelihood that Bold Mission Thrust will become a life-saving reality for the lost and a life-changing reality for the saved?

Bold Mission Thrust must become an urgent, burning reality in the hearts of God's people before it can become a redemptive experience in the lives of the lost.

Churches of New Testament days had their problems. Review what the Spirit said to some of those churches. The church of Ephesus was admonished for having left its first love and was told, "Remember therefore from whence thou art fallen, and repent, and do the first works; or else I will come unto thee quickly, and will remove thy candlestick out of his place, except thou repent (Rev. 2:5). To the church at Laodicia, the Spirit said: "I know thy works, that thou art neither cold nor hot: I would thou wert cold or hot. So then because thou art lukewarm, and neither cold nor hot, I will spue thee out of my mouth. . . . As many as I love, I rebuke and chasten: be zealous therefore, and repent. (Rev. 3:15-16,19). And to the church at Sardis: "I know what you are doing; you have the reputation of being alive, but in reality you are dead. Wake up, and strengthen what is left, although it is on the very point of dying, for I have not found a thing that you have done complete in the sight of God. So remember what you have received and heard, and continue to obey it, and repent. If you do not wake up, I will come like a thief, and you will never know the hour when I come upon you" (Rev. 3:1-3, Williams).[3]

What is the Spirit saying to your church and mine today? Those New Testament churches were told to repent, to return to their first love, to leave lukewarmness, to strengthen what is left, to remember what they had received and heard, and continue to obey it.

Is the Lord giving us similar admonitions today?

Easter Sunday evening of 1986, our church (Judson Baptist Church in Nashville, Tennessee) heard a moving presentation of *2000 A.D.*, a combination of music, Scripture, and drama that lays out clearly the mission of God's people to share the gospel and the love of Christ with people everywhere, to the limit of their abilities. The pastor, H. Raymond Langlois, followed that presentation with a message in which he questioned whether Southern Baptists, and our church, are really serious about Bold Mission Thrust. He said:

> I don't think that we'll be ready when the year 2000 comes unless we make some drastic changes. I am suggesting to you that we will not be ready for Bold Mission Thrust and the year 2000 and all the challenges it brings because there is something dramatically and drastically wrong with our hearts. Our hearts are not right with God. There's a great gap between our profession and our performance! Our real problem is those deterrents [indifference about missions, unconcern for the lost, lack of prayer in our lives]. Folks, there's something wrong in our heart relationship with God, or we would care. People *do* need the Lord! Jesus *does save*! But somehow we have become so comfortable in our pew and our place that we simply don't care!
>
> I would mention another thing, and that is our *duty*. In Matthew 24:14, "And this gospel of the kingdom shall be preached in all the world for a witness unto all nations; and then shall the end come." [Whether] the year 2000 or the return of our Lord [comes first], we are not ready. We have been given a duty to preach the gospel to the world.
>
> I think Bold Mission Thrust is a revelation and a challenge from God. And we accepted it openly; we threw up our arms and said: "Wonderful! Let's take on the challenge!" . . . But dear friends, we are losing the world at a more rapid rate than we were when Bold Mission Thrust was announced. Half the world today, over two billion people, have never heard the name of Jesus. What is our duty? To preach it, to send it, to go if God calls—to do the extraordinary as a church for missions around the world and in our own place where we are. To win our neighbor, the next-door neighbor, the one in our family, the prospect down the street, the one with whom we work. It is our duty, our responsibility to share the message.

Let me offer you a dare. In 2 Chronicles a dare is offered to us, usually associated with revivals; but I think it applies to missions as well. "If my people, which are called by my name, shall humble themselves, and pray, and seek my face, and turn from their wicked ways; then will I hear from heaven, and will forgive their sin, and will heal their land (7:14).

I think we've got heart trouble, folks; and I don't think any Band-Aid is going to fix it. Our slogans about Bold Mission Thrust and all the things we talk about are not going to accomplish a thing in this world unless we take the dare to do what God says. Unless we let Him do what was talked about here awhile ago [in the *2000 A.D.* presentation]—motivate us by His Holy Spirit, change our hearts, dampen our eyes [with tears], bend our knees, and break our hearts over people who are lost, all we are going to do is talk. We like that which relates to me and mine and ours, and that's good, but we really don't care about missions.

If my people, the people who out of the billions in this world do know the name of Christ and have claimed him as Lord and Savior—if my people will humble themselves. Do you know what it means to humble. It's to fall down before God and confess our inadequacies, our coldness, our indifference, and our unconcern.

If we will humble ourselves and pray, I am confident that God will send His Holy Spirit to empower us to be witnesses here in Jerusalem, and in Samaria, and further, to the uttermost parts of the earth. And if we will turn from our own wicked ways, turn from our own sins of indifference and unconcern, and seek His face, seek His way and His will and His purpose in our lives, then He will hear from heaven; and I think He will send His Holy Spirit, and our land will be healed, and our people will be healed, and the fields that are white unto harvest will find the laborers going out into that harvest.

. . .

Are *you* ready for AD 2000?

My prayer is tht God will help us not be distracted from His purpose, that we will not be deterred from God's will and purpose in us because of our heart trouble, but that we will take the dare to be God's people and that we will give and pray and go and be His witnesses here and there, wherever there is.[4]

That message pierced straight to the heart of our church's needs related to Bold Mission Thrust. Does it speak to yours also? Are too many of us in a comfortable rut that is leading (or has led) us into the wilderness of unconcern where our mission as God's people has become entangled in a thicket of other interests? The "other interests" may not be sinful in themselves; perhaps some are even noble and Christian, but they keep us from moving forward boldly down the road of obedience and joy in sharing his love through personal witness and ministry wherever our influence can reach.

Southern Baptist agencies, state convention offices, and associations stand ready as never before to help us share Christ. We have more resources than ever before. We have more powerful means of communication than ever before.

The Spirit of the Lord is ready. Our Lord said: "He that believeth on me, the works that I do shall he do also; and greater works than these shall he do. . . . And whatsoever ye shall ask in my name, that will I do, that the Father may be glorified in the Son. If ye shall ask any thing in my name, I will do it" (John 14:12-14).

AD 2000 is only a few years away! When God's people called Southern Baptists are getting ready to "go to church" on Sunday morning, January 2, 2000, how many lost people in the world will have heard the good news of Christ because of our efforts?

Yes, our Lord is ready; His power is available; strong church programs as discussed in this book are available with resources to support them; other resources are available if we are good stewards; the lost are waiting and dying without Christ. But what of God's people? Are we ready to be bold in the power of the Lord? Each of us must answer. Each church must answer. We must determine whether the question mark is replaced with an exclamation point.

Being God's People: a Southern Baptist Church on Bold Mission!

Here are three summary truths for God's people on Bold Mission:
1. People need the Lord.
2. Being God's people means sharing the gospel with the lost.
3. God's people must take the gospel where lost people are instead of expecting them to come and hear it.

People Need the Lord

Ev'ry day they pass me by.
I can see it in their eyes, empty people filled with care,
    headed who knows where.
On they go through private pain, living fear to fear.
Laughter hides the silent cries only Jesus hears.

People need the Lord. People need the Lord.
At the end of broken dreams
He's the open door.
People need the Lord. People need the Lord.
When will we realize people need the Lord?

We are called to take His light to a world where wrong
    seems right.
What could be too great a cost for sharing life with one
    who's lost?

Through His love our hearts can feel all the grief they bear.
They must hear the words of life
Only we can share.

People need the Lord. People need the Lord.
At the end of broken dreams
He's their open door.
People need the Lord. People need the Lord.
When will we realize that we must give our lives,
For people need the Lord. People need the Lord.[5]

---

[1]Jim Newton, "Tanner Says Statistics Indicate SBC Not Racist," Baptist Press Release 88-35, March 13, 1986.

2. J. N. Barnette, *One to Eight* (Nashville: Sunday School Board of the Southern Baptist Convention, 1954), pp. 1-2.

[3]From *The New Testament, a Translation in the Language of the People,* by Charles B. Williams. Copyright 1937 and 1966. Moody Press, Moody Bible Institute of Chicago. Used by permission.

[4]H. Raymond Langlois (Sermon delivered at Judson Baptist Church, Nashville, Tennessee, March 29, 1986).

[5]PEOPLE NEED THE LORD by Phill McHugh and Greg Nelson. © Copyright 1983 by Shepherd's Fold Music and River Oaks Music. All rights reserved. Used by permission.

Suggestions for the Teacher

Preface and Introduction

Before the session, write the complete title and subtitle of the book on the chalkboard (or chart paper or a poster).

1. Begin by asking group members what they think the title *Being God's People* is intended to emphasize. After they answer, summarize the explanation in the introduction.

2. Ask about the meaning of the subtitle. What is the *mission?* What does *bold* mean? Add to the discussion any ideas from the text that are not mentioned by the group.

Chapter 1, "Learning from New Testament Churches"

1. Write these questions on the chalkboard: Who are God's People? What does God expect of His people? Explain why this study should begin by reviewing what the Bible says about God's people and their mission.

2. Ask the group to mention the various descriptions of the church presented in the text. Have the descriptive phrases written on the chalkboard. Discuss each one briefly.

3. Divide those present into groups of three or four. Ask each group to answer this question: What is the work of God's people in today's world? Encourage them to refer to the related material in the book. After about six minutes ask each group to report. Add any ideas they fail to mention.

4. Ask: "Which essential activities are we doing best? Which need strengthening if a church is to be on bold mission?"

5. Briefly review the remaining material in the chapter about church organization and a church's attitude toward organization, church leaders and their qualifications, and types of relationships.

Chapter 2, "Understanding the Needs of Persons"

Before the session ask a group member to prepare a brief report on the spiritual nature and needs of persons, using ideas from this chapter.

1. Write on the chalkboard the title "Understanding the Needs of Persons." Ask, "What does understanding the needs of persons have to do with the work of our church?" Discuss the group's answers and summarize the ideas from the introductory paragraphs of the chapter, including the definition of a *need*.

2. Call for the report on the spiritual nature and needs of persons. Encourage the group to comment or ask questions.

3. Ask group members to help you list other basic needs of persons. Have the types written on the chalkboard and discuss them briefly. Ask the

group to suggest ways a church can meet each type of need.

4. Quickly review the material on personal crises, and ask group members to suggest ways God's people can minister to persons undergoing such crises.

5. Discuss the meaning of *contextual factors*. Ask, "Which of these factors are most significant in our church situation?"

6. Ask group members whether they agree or disagree with the two summary statements in the last paragraph of the chapter.

Chapter 3, "Turning Concern into Purposeful Action"

Before the session, if the church has a formally adopted statement of mission, plan to use it in activity 3. Have chart paper and markers ready for activity 5.

1. Introduce the chapter by summarizing the ideas in the introductory paragraphs.

2. Write on the chalkboard the definition of *intention*. Lead the group to discuss the question, What are our intentions as a church? Ask, "What two broad categories of intentions are mentioned in the chapter?" Draw a vertical line down the center of the chalkboard. Label the left side "Basic Intentions" and the right side "Dated Intentions." Discuss the two categories. Write "Strategies" and "Goals" under "Dated Intentions." Explain that the remainder of the discussion will be about basic intentions.

3. Discuss the reasons for having clearly stated basic intentions. Write "Mission Statement" under "Basic Intentions" and explain what it means. If the church has a mission statement, use it as an example; if not, use the example from the text.

4. Write the term "Church Functions" under "Mission Statement" and discuss its meaning. Ask the group to name the church functions presented in the text. Write them on the chalkboard and discuss the meaning of each.

5. Divide the group into four workgroups. Give each group a sheet of chart paper with the name of a church function at the top. Ask them to list church activities that relate to that function. After about five minutes let the groups put their lists at the front of the room for everyone to study. Note overlaps and discuss the fact that some activities may involve two or more church functions.

6. Write "Church Tasks" on the left side of the chalkboard and briefly explain their meaning and values.

7. Write the three types of programs on the chalkboard under "Church Tasks," and ask the group to name the programs that fall under each type. Explain that the remainder of the book describes the work of these pro-

grams and how their work may be coordinated into a total church program.

Chapter 4, "Leading the Church Through Pastoral Ministries"
Before the session, put on the chalkboard or on a poster the words "Pastoral Ministries" and the program's tasks. Cover the tasks with newsprint or chart paper until you are ready to discuss them. Ask four members to prepare a brief overview of the work included in one of the pastoral ministries tasks and be ready to present it in the session.

1. Call attention to the name of the chapter and ask, "What is the difference between *pastor* and *pastoral*?" Stress the important leadership role of the pastor, and ask, "Who else serves as pastoral ministries leaders?"

2. Explain that pastor, deacons, and other staff members are responsible for four church tasks; and uncover your list. Call on the persons assigned to report on each task. Add ideas if needed. Lead the group to discuss ways each task could be focused on the Bold Mission Thrust objective.

Chapter 5, "Sharing Christ Through Bible Teaching and Outreach"
1. Begin by asking, "What is the purpose of the Sunday School?" If the immediate answer is "to teach the Bible," probe more deeply by asking, "What else is the Sunday School intended to do in a church?" Write each task on the chalkboard as it is mentioned.

2. Ask, "Which of these is a more inclusive name 'Sunday School' or 'Bible teaching program'?" Emphasize that thinking in terms of the broader Bible teaching program concept can help a church find ways to teach the Bible at times and places other than Sunday morning at the church building.

3. Divide those present into five discussion groups (or make individual assignments). Assign one of the first five Bible teaching program tasks to each group (or person). Ask the group (or individual) to prepare a report as follows: (a) Give two examples of activities related to this task in your church. (b) State how well you think the task is being done in your church. (c) Name one thing your Bible teaching program might do in this task area to be more effective in sharing the gospel with the lost.

4. Ask, "Do any of these tasks need to be given higher priority in connection with Bold Mission Thrust?"

Chapter 6, "Equipping God's People Through Discipleship Training"
Before the session, enlist a group member to prepare a five-minute answer to the question, What does it mean to be a disciple? based on the material

in chapter 1. Suggest that a reading of Ephesians 4:11-16 be included.

Write on a poster or chart paper "Church Training" and the six tasks of the program. Leave the tasks covered until they are discussed.

Ask two group members to be ready to share with the group some ways in which participation in Church Training has helped them grow in their discipleship.

1. Comment on the importance of equipping God's people through discipleship training to be effective in fulfilling their mission.

2. Emphasize the need for a biblical understanding of discipleship and call for the report assigned in advance. Reinforce the key ideas and add any other ideas from the text.

3. Summarize the ideas in the section "What Is Our Mandate from God?" Stress the importance of continuing growth in the life of the individual Christian and of the church. Call on the two members enlisted in advance to share ways in which Church Training has helped them grow. Invite others to share also.

4. Reveal the Church Training tasks and ask, "Is there a task here that you do not usually think of as a Church Training responsibility?" Describe briefly what each task includes. Invite members to share information from the text. Ask: "How well are these tasks being done in our church? Do any of them need more attention if the church is to be well-equipped for bold mission?"

5. Call attention to Roy Edgemon's dream for the future of discipleship training in the churches. Ask, "What dream or intentions does our church have about equipping its members for bold discipleship?

Chapter 7, "Involving God's People Through the Music Ministry"

Before the session, put the words "Music Ministry" and its tasks on a poster or chart paper and leave the tasks covered until called for in the discussion.

1. Invite members of the group to mention ways music has contributed to their lives and to their church.

2. Ask, "What are the responsibilities (tasks) of the Music Ministry?" As tasks are mentioned, uncover them on the poster. After all have been mentioned ask, "Were any of these tsks less familiar to you as part of the Music Ministry's assignment?

3. Ask the group to brainstorm (list without evaluating) ways music could be used by their church in witness and ministry to the lost. List ideas on the chalkboard. Ask the group to pick three ideas that are most promising as possibilities for their church.

Chapter 8, "Sharing God's Love Through Missions"

Before the session, prepare posters or chart paper giving the name and tasks of the three programs discussed in this chapter. Leave the tasks covered until they are discussed.

Ask a group member to review the current church budget and be ready to report (1) the total amount the church is giving to missions, (2) the amount given locally, through the association, through the Cooperative Program, and to any other missions activities beyond the church's immediate needs, and (3) the percentage of the total budget that is committed to missions.

Ask the directors of Woman's Missionary Union, Brotherhood, and Missions Development (or missions committee chairman) to come to your group to give about a seven-minute overview of each program's tasks, the missions activities and projects currently in progress, and those planned for the future and to remain for the discussion as resource persons. If your church does not have one of these programs, ask a group member to summarize the work of the program, using information in the text and information about any missions activities the church may be involved in.

1. Call attention to the quotation that begins chapter 8, and discuss the fundamental importance of missions in a church's mission and in Southern Baptists' Bold Mission Thrust. Explain that the three programs presented in this chapter can help a church be aggressively and effectively involved in missions.

2. Introduce the program directors who have come (or the assigned individuals), and ask for their reports. As programs are discussed, reveal the tasks on the chart. After all three speak, invite questions or comments from the group, and involve the program directors in answering them.

3. Call for the report about the budget. Ask, "What does our budget indicate about our church's commitment to missions?"

4. Lead the group to identify and list on the chalkboard specific things the church and its members might do to express a greater commitment to missions in connection with Bold Mission Thrust. Have prayer about the church's involvement in missions.

Chapter 9, "Reaching Persons for Christ"

1. Call attention to the quote from Robert Hamblin of the Home Mission Board. Explain that this chapter describes how reaching people for Christ—evangelism—can be made a priority concern of the church as the efforts of basic and other church programs are built into a churchwide strategy for evangelism developed with the leadership and assistance of the

evangelism council, working through the Church Council.

2. Ask the group to review the list of basic church program tasks that relate to reaching people for Christ and the tasks of the evangelism program. List the evangelism program tasks on the chalkboard. Explain that these tasks and the organization for the program have been strengthened in recent years in an effort to help churches give biblical priority to evangelism.

3. Divide the group into three workgroups. Assign one evangelism program task to each group. Ask the group to take about eight minutes to study their task and prepare a summary of the work it includes. Ask for the group reports and discuss them.

4. Lead the group to identify which evangelism program tasks and basic program tasks relating to evangelism the church has organization to accomplish. Ask, "What are some specific ways our church could give higher priority to reaching the lost for Christ?"

Chapter 10, "Providing for Essential Church Concerns"

Before the session, enlist four group members to prepare a brief report describing the task(s) of one of these programs and giving an overview of how the program does its work (methods, organization, relationships with other programs, etc.).

1. Remind the group about the nature of an emphasis program. Write on the chalkboard the names of the four programs discussed in the chapter. Emphasize the second paragraph in the chapter which describes how an emphasis program can help a church strengthen its work in the area of emphasis concern.

2. Call for the reports on each program. Add additional material if needed, and encourage the group to ask questions for discussion.

3. Ask, "Which of these emphasis programs are most effective in our church and which one(s) may need more attention?"

Chapter 11, "Helping a Church Function Effectively"

Before the session, write on the chalkboard (or poster) the heading "Service Programs," and then list "Media Library," "Recreation Services," and "Administrative Services."

If your church has designated a leader (layperson or staff member) for these programs, invite that person to present the work of the program and remain as a resource person.

1. Ask, "Why is there a need for service programs in a church?" Supplement answers from the group with material from the introduction to the chapter and to the section on each program.

2. Give an overview of the services a media library program can provide for a church (or have the media library representative do it).

3. Lead the group to search their texts to identify the various types of church recreation. List these on the chalkboard or chart paper as they are identified. (If a recreation representative was enlisted, call on him or her to comment on the work of the program and assist in the discussion.) Lead the group to identify three ways recreation could be used in outreach, witnessing, and/or ministry in the community.

4. Lead the group to discuss the question, Why does a church need administrative services? Ask, "Who is responsible for making the decisions necessary to plan, manage, and govern the affairs of a Southern Baptist church?" Lead the group to list the officers and committees their church has. (If a representative of administrative services is present, let him or her help lead the discussion.)

Chapter 12, "Coordinating a Church's Work"

1. Ask the group, "What would happen if each program leader planned the work of that program without checking with any of the others about their plans?" Point out that the answers to this queston suggest why coordination is needed. Call attention to additional reasons why coordination is needed.

2. Ask the group to identify three levels of coordination and to determine which of them their church has.

3. Lead the group to identify and list on the chalkboard those who usually serve on a Church Council as listed in the text. Discuss what a Church Council can do for a church.

Chapter 13, "Being God's People: a Southern Baptist Church on Bold Mission?"

Lead the group in evaluating their church program by asking questions like those in the paragraph beginning, "Let's think about your church and mine." Ask them to consider whether the book title should be followed by a question mark or an exclamation point at present with reference to their church. Close with prayer asking for God's guidance and strength in leading the church to be on bold mission as never before.

The Church Study Course

The Church Study Course is a Southern Baptist educational system consisting of short courses for adults and youth combined with a credit and recognition system. More than 600 courses are available in 24 subject areas. Credit is awarded for each course completed. These credits may be applied to one or more of the 135 diplomas in the recognition system. Diplomas are available for most leadership positions as well as general diplomas for all Christians. These diplomas are the certification that a person has completed from 5 to 8 prescribed courses. Diploma requirements are given in the catalog.

Complete details about the Church Study Course system, courses available, and diplomas offered may be found in a current copy of the *Church Study Course Catalog.* Study Course materials are available from Baptist Book Stores.

The Church Study Course system is sponsored by the Sunday School Board, Woman's Missionary Union, and Brotherhood Commission of the Southern Baptist Convention.

How to Request Credit for This Course

This book is the text for course number 01020 in the subject area: "The Church." This course is designed for a minimum of 5 hours of group study; 8 hours is recommended.

Credit for this course may be obtained in two ways:

1. Read the book and attend class sessions. (If you are absent from one or more sessions, complete the "Personal Learning Activities" for the material missed.)

2. Read the book and complete the "Personal Learning Activities." (Written work should be submitted to an appropriate church leader.)

A request for credit may be made on Form 725 "Church Study Course Enrollment/Credit Request" and sent to the Awards Office, Sunday School Board, 127 Ninth Avenue, North, Nashville, Tennessee 37234. The form on the following page may be used to request credit.

A record of your awards will be maintained by the Awards Office.

CHURCH STUDY COURSE
ENROLLMENT/CREDIT REQUEST
FORM - 725 (Rev. 1-89)

MAIL THIS REQUEST TO ▲

CHURCH STUDY COURSE AWARDS OFFICE
BAPTIST SUNDAY SCHOOL BOARD
127 NINTH AVENUE, NORTH
NASHVILLE, TENNESSEE 37234

Is this the first course taken since 1983? ☐ YES If yes, or not sure complete all of Section 1. ☐ NO If no, complete only bold boxes in Section 1.

SECTION 1 - STUDENT I.D.

Social Security Number | — | — | — |

☐ Mr. ☐ Miss
☐ Mrs.

Personal CSC Number* | — | — | — | ▲

DATE OF BIRTH | Month | — | Day | — | Year

Name (First, MI, Last)

Street, Route, or P.O. Box

City, State | Zip Code

Church Name

Mailing Address

City, State | Zip Code

STUDENT

CHURCH

SECTION 2 - CHANGE REQUEST ONLY (Current inf. in Section1)

☐ Former Name | Zip Code

☐ Former Address | Zip Code

☐ Former Church | Zip Code

SECTION 3 - COURSE CREDIT REQUEST

Course No.	Title (use exact title)
1. 01020	Being God's People: a Southern Baptist Church on Bold Mission
2.	
3.	
4.	
5.	
6.	

SECTION 4 - DIPLOMA ENROLLMENT

Enter exact diploma title from current Church Study Course catalog. Indicate diploma age group if appropriate. Do not enroll again with each course. When all requirements have been met, the diploma will be mailed to your church. Enrollment in Christian Development Diplomas is automatic. No charge will be made for enrollment or diplomas.

Title of Diploma	Age group or area
Title of Diploma	Age group or area
Signature of Pastor, Teacher, or Other Church Leader	Date

*CSC # not required for new students. Others please give CSC # when using SS # for the first time. Then, only one ID # is required.